A CHARTWELL-BRATT STUDENT TEXT

C Simply

An introduction to C Programming

Mike Parr

Department of Computer Studies
Sheffield Polytechnic

Chartwell-Bratt Studentlitteratur

British Library Cataloguing in Publication Data
Parr, Mike
C simply
1. Computer systems. Programming languages: C language
I. Title
005.133

ISBN 0-86238-262-9

All rights reserved. No part of this publication may be reproduced or transmitted in any form or by any means, electronic or mechanical, including photocopying, recording, or any information storage and retrieval system, without permission in writing from the publisher.

© Mike Parr and Chartwell-Bratt Ltd, 1990

Chartwell-Bratt (Publishing and Training) Ltd
ISBN 0-86238-262-9

Printed in Sweden,
Studentlitteratur, Lund
ISBN 91-44-33001-4

1 2 3 4 5 6 7 8 9 10 | 1994 93 92 91 90

CONTENTS

PREFACE

This book aims to teach a subset of the C programming language, and is suitable for introductory study at any level. It assumes no previous knowledge, and the pace is gentle.

The text is not oriented towards a particular version of C – the most widespread one is covered, but note is also taken of the new ANSI C standard.

Though C is very popular, being used to write software ranging from databases to word-processors, the range of possible constructs means that the beginner is advised to start on a subset of the whole language: this approach is taken here. Where appropriate, chapters have a 'Big Picture' section to take the reader beyond the subset.

Chapters 1 and 2 (on top-down design) should be read by all, but not dwelt on. However it would be useful to re-read them after chapter 8 has been covered.

CHAPTER 1

AN INTRODUCTION TO PROGRAM DESIGN

Introduction

The term 'design' has an artistic and commercial aura – an electrical manufacturing company might say "what should our new kettle look like? How is it to be filled? What colour? Can it be misused or damaged? What social class of person will desire it?". The design of programs is in the main concerned with different questions, but one property is common. A good product is reliable and does the job for which it is intended.

Consider a computer program – a sequence of instructions for a computer, e.g:

```
for each employee:
    find hours worked by employee
    calculate gross pay
    print pay slip
    subtract deductions
```

Large programs may consist of 100,000 lines of such instructions, with a high probability that errors ('bugs') will creep in. Did you spot the error above ? The deductions should be subtracted before printing the pay slip.

Typically, large software systems are planned by a software designer, who takes an abstract view of the task. (In computer jargon, 'abstraction' involves extracting the essence of a problem, whilst ignoring insignificant detail.) The resulting plan is then passed to a programmer or coder who translates it into a programming language – e.g. C. However, when we are dealing with relatively small programs, one individual may do both jobs. Similarly, in educational establishments, students may have to design and code a program.

1.1 The Software Life – cycle

Imagine the phases that a product (e.g. a car) passes through:

feasibility study
design
testing
selling
maintenance

The last phase might involve setting up and maintaining a spares network for say ten years. Consider also the possibility that, because of an error in design, a fault exists in the brakes of every car. This involves a major expenditure, as every owner must be contacted and instructed to return the car for servicing. The life – cycle of a large software system is similar. It will inevitably contain bugs, and these are expensive to correct. In fact, studies of large systems reveal that over 50% of the cost is involved with maintenance. This cost might be reduced if we spend longer on the design stage, because bugs found here are cheaper to fix. Financial considerations are not the only motive. Consider patient – monitoring systems or nuclear power station control systems. Bugs here are life – threatening, not merely expensive!

1.2 Top – down Design

Consider the variety of programs that we might want to design:

video game
power station control system
payroll program
spreadsheet
missile detection and launching system
etc

There are numerous design methods, and proponents of each method will tell you that theirs is the best for a particular type of program. This text is mainly concerned with C programming, but we shall look at one particular approach - top-down design (often called 'stepwise refinement'). The method has two important aspects:

- splitting a problem up into several easier problems
- suppressing insignificant detail.

1.3 Pseudocode Algorithms

An 'algorithm' is a series of steps that solve a problem. For example, a knitting pattern, a recipe, a pseudocode design and a C program are examples of algorithms. It is a general term for a plan; in the early stage of producing a program, we 'design the algorithm'.

We shall use a popular method of expressing designs known as 'pseudocode' - a mixture of programming language and English language. We have a means of expressing:

sequence	–	one step after another.
subtasks	–	a sub-problem of the complete problem.
selection	–	choosing between alternatives.
repetition	–	repeating tasks until something happens.
variables	–	remembering values.

For certain problems it may be neccessary to express the concept of input/output, but this is not crucial in the early stages of learning design.

Pseudocode is not a programming language in itself, more a means of planning a solution, which will eventually be converted into C. In fact the above five concepts are present in most programming languages, so our pseudocode design will be useful whichever language we adopt. Note however that many of the problems posed at the end of each chapter are small, and the approach described here is more appropriate to larger problems.

1.4 Sequence

Throughout this introduction to design, we will use the example of instructing a robot chef in how to prepare a Chinese meal. To express sequence, we write the tasks in order, e.g:

```
chop meat
chop vegetables
stir-fry in wok          (a wok is a large oriental pan!)
add vegetables
add sauce
serve up
```

Our assumption is that the first instruction to be obeyed is 'chop meat' and the last one is 'serve up'.

1.5 Subtasks – functions

Sub-tasks are known as functions in C. In other languages they are termed subroutines, procedures, paragraphs, sub-programs, etc. Clearly, 'chop vegetables' itself consists of several steps, which we can write as:

```
chop vegetables consists of
    peel garlic
    chop garlic
    peel onion
    chop onion
end of function
```

It is important to show the end of the function (subtask) because we may have several on one page.

In general, we write a pseudocode function in the form of:

```
???? consists of          ( ???? is the name of the function)
    task 1
    task 2
    etc

end of function
```

1.6 Selection

We use the keywords 'if', 'else' and 'endif' to show a choice between two alternatives, as in:

```
if more than four diners
    use large wok
else
    use medium wok
endif
add oil to wok
```

It is important to line up the three keywords and to indent (move to the right) the options that they contain, making it easier for us to read and check the logic.

Following the word 'if' we must put a condition, which our robot chef will find to be true or false. If it is true, a large wok will be used. If it is false, a medium wok will be used. In either case, the next instruction to be obeyed will be the one following the 'endif' (i.e. add oil to wok.)

Note:

- The two options can contain any number of instructions.
- If 'else' sounds awkward, interpret it as 'otherwise'.
- The second option might not be needed in certain problems, so we may put e.g:

```
if peas are frozen
    defrost peas
else
    do nothing
endif
```

The general form of a pseudocode 'if' is:

```
if condition
    task 1          ( done when true )
    task 2
    etc
else
    task 3          ( done when false )
    task 4
    etc
endif
```

1.7 Repetition

We use the concept of repeating a task as long as a certain condition remains true. Here is an example:

```
mix sauce ingredients
while sauce is too thick
    add more water
    stir
endwhile
pour sauce over food
```

The representation of the above as a flowchart is:

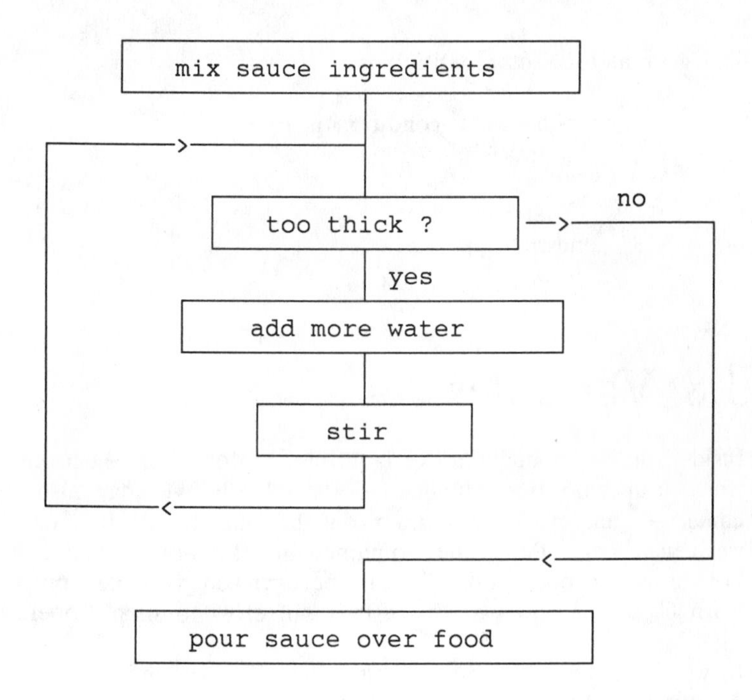

'While' is an important concept, perhaps not as natural to our way of thinking as 'if'. Properly used, it is very powerful.

Note:

- 'while' means 'as long as'

- 'add more water' and 'stir' are obeyed again and again, as long as it is true that the sauce is too thick. When this condition becomes false, the algorithm continues with the statement immediately below the 'endwhile'.

- the condition for going through the loop is tested at the top of the loop. In our example, if the sauce happened to be perfect immediately after mixing the sauce ingredients, then the 'while' condition would be false, the loop would not be entered, and the next task would be ' pour sauce over food'.

- for readability, we indent the tasks in the middle (i.e. the 'body') of the loop.

The general form of repetition is:

```
while  some condition is true
    task1
    task2
    etc
endwhile
```

1.8 Variables

Inside the computer, a variable is a form of electronic storage box, which can hold one number – its value. We may also give the box a name – imagine it is written on the outside of the box. At any time, we can change the value contained in the box, but not its name. The full range of operations we can perform on variables must wait until we learn C, so for now we will restrict ourselves to simple operations.

If we have two variables, arbitrarily called x and y, we may use simple instructions of the form:

```
set x to 1          (put 1 in box x)
set y to 6          (put 6 in box y)
add 2 to x          (x is now 3)
add 9 to y          (y is now 15, x is still 3)
add x to y          (y is now 18, x is still 3)
```

We may also test the contents of boxes in 'if' and 'while'.

For example, to instruct out robot chef to stir the soup 10 times we could put:

```
set count to 0
while count less than 10
    stir once
    add 1 to count
endwhile
```

This is a very common pattern in programming. We invent a variable called 'count', and set it to 0. As long as its value is less than 10, we stir once, and remember this by adding 1 into count. Eventually, count will tick up to 10, and the loop will finish. If we could look at the value of count as we were stirring, we would see it take the following sequence of values:

0 1 2 3 4 5 6 7 8 9

i.e the loop is performed 10 times (count them !) in all.

Note:

- variables keep their value until we explicitly change them.
- you must put a value in a variable before making use of the value. Don't assume that the contents will automatically be zero.

1.9 Example : The pile of cards

Imagine a pile of cards, with a number (positive or negative) printed on each one. We are allowed to pick up the top card (when the pile is not empty) and use its value . We will assume that initially there is at least one card, but will occasionally consider the possibility that the pile is initially empty.

The analogy is with a data file containing a series of numbers. The file may sometimes be empty (e.g. the file may contain details of students who failed an exam in C programming).

Problem 1: design a pseudocode algorithm to count how many cards are in the pile.

A solution:

```
set count to 0
while pile not empty
    pick up card
    add 1 to count
endwhile
```

We have invented a variable called 'count'. Each time it is possible to pick up a card, we count it. The variable ends up containing the number of cards. It will also be correct if the pile was initially empty.

Problem 2: design a pseudocode algorithm to count the number of cards which have 999 printed on them.

A solution:

```
set count to 0
while pile not empty
    pick up card
    if value on card is 999
        add 1 to count
    else
        ignore card
    endif
endwhile
```

Note that the if/endif is completely nested within while/endwhile. The following is incorrect:

```
while ...
    if

    else

endwhile

    endif
```

As an alternative, we could have split the algorithm into two tasks, as in:

```
set count to 0
while pile not empty
    pick up card
    check 999
endwhile

check 999 consists of:
    if value on card is 999
        add 1 to count
    else
        ignore card
    endif
end of function
```

Problem 3: add up all the numbers on the cards.

A solution:

```
set sum to 0
while pile not empty
    pick up card
    add number on card to sum
endwhile
```

Note: the variable called sum is a running total, while builds up the sum as the data is processed. We could reasonably have called it

total   running total   sum of cards

but not

x   y   s   result

because these names don't convey the purpose of the program.

Key Points

- Pseudocode uses the concepts of sequence, subtasks, selection, repetition, and variables.

- Pseudocode cannot be directly understood by computers – it needs to be converted to a more detailed programming language.

- The pseudocode solutions shown are not the only possible ones, and were the result of several discarded attempts. Don't expect to write down perfect solutions immediately.

- Top–down design needs experience – at first it is difficult to know which subtasks to choose. Re–read the two design chapters again after you have written some small programs.

Problems

The following problems are based on the pile of numbered cards.

1. Design a pseudocode algorithm to find the sum of all the positive numbers on the cards.

2. Assuming that there is at least one card on the pile, design a pseudocode algorithm to find the largest of all the numbers on the cards. (n.b. in Mathematics, largest means 'most positive', so -5 is bigger than -8).

3. Assuming that there is at least one card on the pile, design a pseudocode algorithm to find whether the pile contains an odd or even number of cards.

4. Assuming that there is at least one card on the pile, design a pseudocode algorithm to find the average of all the numbers on the cards.

CHAPTER 2
FURTHER DESIGN

Introduction

In the previous chapter, we used pseudocode to tackle simple problems – there was no real need to break the problem up into sub-problems. In this chapter we will look at a larger problem involving tickets for a underground transport system, in which we will be forced to think at a high level.

Our first problem however will involve the use the use of complicated conditions in 'while' loops. This is very common in programming but unfortunately it is easy to express the conditions incorrectly, carrying over incorrect English statements into pseudocode and then into C, with disastrous results!

2.1 Combining Conditions

We have seen that conditions (which will end up as true or false) must be used following 'while' and 'if'. However, we may need to <u>combine</u> conditions, as in:

```
if  mark greater or equal to 0
    and  mark less than or equal to 100

    mark is valid (i.e.  between 0 to 100 )
else
    mark is incorrect
endif
```

Here, we have combined two conditions with 'and'. Should we have put 'or' instead?

We will return to this later. Consider the statement:

'I'll drink anything if it is hot and sweet!'.

There is a main condition formed from two subsiduary conditions. The use of 'and' means that the drink must be both hot and sweet. If only one of these conditions is false, the complete condition is false. What if we had mistakenly put 'hot or sweet'? We would now drink it in these cases:

hot only
sweet only
hot and sweet

Returning to our marks problem, it is not sufficient that our mark is greater or equal to zero (e.g. 5, 45, 99, 123 ..). It must also be less than or equal to 100. Both conditions must apply, so 'and' is correct.

Let us look at 'while' with combined conditions. The most common form is when the loop is to end when any one of a series of conditions changes from true to false. Imagine a person searching for some dropped money when it is getting dark:

'I'll keep looking as long it is light and I haven't found it.'

'And' has been used correctly to combine the conditions. In pseudocode we could put:

```
while money not found  and  still daylight
     keep looking
endwhile
```

Here, any one of the two conditions turning false will stop the loop – they must both be true to continue looking. In English, we often use 'or' instead of 'and'. In programming, analyse combined conditions carefully!

2.2 CD Example

We are going to design some software to control a robot compact disc finder. The setup is as follows:

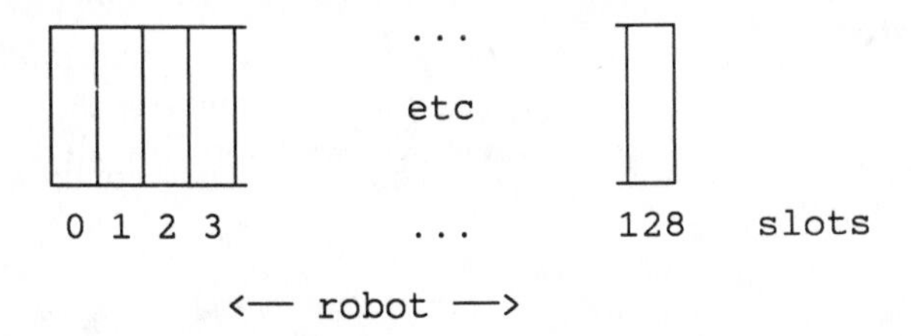

We have a rack containing 128 CD's in random order, and a robot hand which can be programmed to scan along the rack and stop when the required CD is found. Slot 0 is empty, and is the 'home' position. The robot is clever in that it can read the title of the CD it is positioned at, but stupid in that it can only obey these simple instructions:

go home (to slot 0)

move one place right

In case you think that this has nothing to do with computer programming, note that it is a close analogy. The rack is a data file, a CD is a single data item, and we will be producing some software to search the data.

Problem 1. Our music fan requires that the robot searches for Bruce Springsteen's 'Nebraska' CD, stopping at the appropriate slot.

A Solution:

```
go home              (i.e.  start at left )
move one place right
while current CD is not 'Nebraska'
     move one place right
endwhile
```

This works after a fashion, but what if the CD is missing? Presumably the robot will crash into the right hand edge of the rack. We could improve the algorithm by incorporating an additional condition:

```
go home                (i.e.  start at left )
move one place right
while current CD is not 'Nebraska'  and  not reached right of rack
    move one place right
endwhile
```

We need to be careful with the and/or choice. The condition for continuing to search is that:

```
    current CD is not 'Nebraska'            is  true
and
    not reached right of rack               is  true
```

When any one of these becomes false, the loop should be ended.

Problem 2. We require that the same CD is located but, if it is missing, the robot should return to 'home'.

Refer to the previous solution for problem 1. Immediately below the 'endwhile', we need to find out which of the two conditions caused the loop to finish. We could use an 'if', as shown below.

A Solution:

```
go home                (i.e.  start at left )
move one place right
while current CD is not 'Nebraska'  and  not reached right of rack
    move one place right
endwhile
if at right of rack
    go home
else
    do nothing
endif
```

This is one of several solutions. Here is another one which uses a variable which we set to 0 (false) or 1 (true) to indicate whether the CD has been found:

```
go home              (i.e.  start at left )
set found to 0
move one place right
while  found is 0   and  not reached right of rack
    if current CD is 'Nebraska'
        set found to 1
    else
        move one place right
    endif
endwhile
if found is 0
    go home
else
    do nothing
endif
```

2.3 Transport Example

This example is considerably more abstract than what has gone before – intentionally so to show the approach of top–down design, in which we split a large task into several smaller tasks, and also try to ignore insignificant detail.

The problem is concerned with a new underground transport system on the island of Singakong. It is intended that passengers buy tickets containing a magnetic strip, onto which data can be placed ('written') and recalled ('read'). We are going to design some software which will be installed in three pieces of machinery: ticket dispensers, entry gates, and exit gates.

A complete and accurate specification for the software would be rather lengthy, but here are some of the main features:

There are two types of ticket which can be bought from dispensers:

- one–trip tickets costing 10 or 50 cents (depending on the length of the journey)
- multi–trip tickets costing 2 dollars, which can be used again and again on 10 and 50 cent journeys – they are more convenient.

At the exit gate, one-trip tickets will be kept inside the machine, but multi-trip tickets will be returned to the traveller. If the ticket won't pay for the journey, the gate will remain closed and an alarm will sound.

At the entry gate, the ticket is passed through a machine, which writes the name of the station onto the ticket. At this point, we don't require the destination - the calculation of the cost of the journey (10 or 50 cents) will be done at the exit gate.

Let's look at the logic for dispensing tickets. The machine will continually wait for coins and issue tickets - i.e a looping structure. We could put:

```
while machine still holds tickets
    wait for money
    dispense appropriate ticket
endwhile
display an "out of tickets" message


dispense appropriate ticket   consists of:
    if money is 10 cents
        dispense 10 cent ticket
    else
        if money is 50 cents
            dispense 50 cent ticket
        else
            if money is 2 dollars
                dispense multi-trip ticket
            else
                display a "wrong money" message
                eject money
            endif
        endif
    endif
end of function
```

Note that a function has been used - this was not essential but it enables us to focus on one part. Additionally, we are ignoring details - how does the machine recognise when a coin is entered, and how is the denomination of the coin detected? The top-down viewpoint is that the inclusion of such details at this early stage could clutter-up the basic logic.

Moving on to the entry gate. We can arrange for the gate to write a station I.D. on each ticket, to enable the exit gate to calculate the length of the journey.

```
while subway operating
    wait for ticket
    write station I.D on ticket
    eject ticket
    open gate
endwhile
```

Now for the exit gate. One–trip tickets are not returned to the traveller, but multi–trip tickets may be if they are not used up.

```
while subway operating
    shut gate
    wait for ticket
    read amount and station I.D from ticket
    compute cost of trip
    set reduced amount to  amount on ticket  minus  cost of trip
    if reduced amount less than 0
        sound alarm  –  not enough value on ticket
    else
        process correct ticket
    endif
endwhile
```

```
process correct ticket  consists of:
    if ticket is one–trip (10 or 50)
        keep in machine
    else
        if reduced amount equals 0
            keep in machine
        else
            write reduced amount onto ticket
            eject ticket
        endif
    endif
    open gate
end of function
```

This concludes the top-level logic of the design.

Key Points

- Check and/or conditions carefully.
- Split large tasks into smaller tasks.

Problems

1. Design an algorithm which instructs someone how to make a phone call. Assume that the phone could be damaged and the number could be engaged.

The following problems are based on the CD system.

2. Design some pseudocode to search for the 'Nebraska' CD, given that the CDs are now in <u>alphabetic</u> order, and the robot can deal with conditions such as:

    while current CD <u>before</u> 'Nebraska'

3. As Q2 - the CDs are in alphabetic order, but the robot can now go directly to any disc position, e.g:

    set n to 64
    move to n'th CD

    (Try to locate the disc in the <u>minimum</u> number of attempts.)

CHAPTER 3
COMPUTERS – THE BASICS

Introduction

The purpose of this chapter is to provide an introduction to the considerable amount of jargon in computing. Though this book is mainly concerned with writing C programs, the actual use of computer systems requires the ability to understand technical literature. This comes with experience, but here a brief overview is presented.

3.1 Hardware

The term 'hardware' refers to the physical end electronic parts of a computer. The main components are:

- The keyboard. Of particular significance are the keys marked 'return' (or 'enter'), and 'shift'. The 'return' key is used to signify that the line you have typed is complete – imagine that the line is transmitted to the computer when this key is pressed. The 'shift' key is used by holding it down whilst pressing other keys. It is used to produce 'upper case' letters A to Z (as opposed to lower case a to z) and to produce the upper symbol on many keys(e.g. '(' instead of '9').

- The screen, with a flashing dot called the cursor. This shows the current typing position, and can be moved by 'cursor – control' keys (typically with arrows on them) or, on more modern machines, by a mouse which, when moved by hand, moves the screen cursor correspondingly. Some machines also can display information in different areas of the screen, rather like sheets of paper on a desk. These areas are called windows.

- The disc drive. On large computer systems, the disc storage may be behind the scenes, but on personal systems, programmers will use cheap discs which can be inserted and removed via the drive slot. However, they are not 100% reliable, so backup duplicate copies should be kept. As a rough guide, the contents of this book could be stored on one disc.

  The storage area on a disc can be split up into areas called directories – each directory can hold several files. As an example, we might create two directories:

  letters
  programs

  In the letters directory, we might have two files:

  job application
  complaint

  In the programs directory we might have three files:

  game.c
  game.o
  personal finance

  Inside the 'game.c' file, we might have a C program, and in game.o we would have the machine code (object code) version. Each file and directory is given a brief name by the programmer. The exact rules for forming names (whether spaces or hyphens can be used, etc.) vary from computer to computer.

- Chips. Inside the computer there are two types of micro–chips:

  RAM – random access memory

  CPU – central processor unit.

When we use C commands such as:

```
x = n+1;
```

the values of x and n are held in RAM, and the CPU performs the actual addition. To give you a feel for the scale, a typical RAM will be able to hold one million numbers, and an addition will take one – millionth of a second.

3.2 Software

Software is harder to describe – it is less tangible than hardware. Imagine some written instructions for finding your way to a destination. The streets and buses are the hardware, and the instructions are the software. You could even memorise the instructions and throw them away – you still have the plan in your mind!

To take the analogy further, we can also make the distinction between the instructions kept unused in your pocket, and the instructions when you are in the act of using them. In computer terms, the instructions are a program which can be stored on disc. To actually obey the program, it is loaded into RAM, and executed (or 'run') by the CPU. In this section, we will look at some important software concepts.

- Machine code (object code). The CPU can only interpret instructions written in machine code. In principle, we could use this language to write programs, but it is very tedious and error – prone. For example, the calculation:

  ```
  x-y+z
  ```

  would be carried out in machine – code by instructions of the form:

  ```
  fetch x value
  fetch y value
  subtract them
  fetch z value
  add it
  ```

  To avoid these very low – level instructions, we use a C compiler to translate C statements into machine code, which can then be executed. In short, C programs have to be compiled (translated) before running.

- The Operating System. This is a large program which usually stays in RAM, alongside every other program. It handles such tasks as:

  - file handling (creating, deleting, moving, printing ...)
  - interpreting the user's keyboard commands.
  - running other programs.

Whichever operating system you use, the following pattern of commands is common:

1. Type in or amend your C program with an editor.
2. Compile the program.
3. If compilation errors occur, go to step 1 and amend.
4. Execute the program. If errors occur, go to 1. and amend.

Here, three programs are being executed: editor, compiler, and C program. With some operating systems, each of these is initiated by a (potentially) complicated command. Alternatively, you may have a C 'environment', in which a single key-press will do the job.

Note the possibility of errors in the above steps. In fact, certainty is more appropriate. There are two general categories, called compilation (or syntax) errors, and run-time errors (bugs). A compilation error is akin to a spelling mistake - you won't make very many when you get used to the language, and they are usually easy to locate. Run-time errors are typically caused because the logic of the program is wrong i.e. it is grammatically correct but doesn't carry out the intended task. Spotting these takes time and patience. Some operating systems will provide a collection of programs called 'software tools', to assist in the process of programming , and one of these tools is likely to be a debugger. With the aid of a debugger, you can execute your program a step at a time and trace its logic.

3.3 A First Program

Enough of words - now for action! You need to get to grips with your system sooner or later, so here is a C program, which you could type in by using the editor. You might store it in a file called first.c

Note that you would not type the line numbers at the right - they are to assist in the explanation.

```
/*  my first C program  */                  (1)
#include <stdio.h>                          (2)
main()                                      (3)
{                                           (4)
   printf( "Hello\nWorld!\n" );             (5)
}                                           (6)
```

When you type the appropriate commands to compile and run the program, you will find that it displays the following on the screen:

```
Hello
World!
```

Here, some introductory points are covered, to be explained in more depth later.

Line 1 shows a comment enclosed in /* */
Comments can contain any text whatsoever, without any rules. They help someone else to follow the program. An analogy is jottings made in the margins of your notes, to clarify their meaning.

line 2 is necessary in most C programs. You don't need to know exactly what it does at this stage.

Line 3 is necessary in most small C programs - the program actually starts running at this line.

Lines 4 and 6 are 'braces' - { } . They group statements together. Note that in C we also have parentheses (round brackets) and later we will encounter [ ] - square brackets.

Line 5 shows the 'formatted print' function to used print out some text on the screen. It prints exactly what is between the quotes, except when we use '\n', which it interprets as meaning 'start a new line'. There are two similar characters – / and \ – make sure you get the correct one. Also, we obtain the " character by pressing one key, rather than two single quotes.

The semicolon ends every statement – the problem is that every line of the above is not technically a statement so you can't litter semicolons around with abandon.

Typing in 6 lines of program sounds easy, but if you are new to computers it is not! Everyone finds it hard at first but after a few sessions, the keyboard and editor will become familiar.

Key Points

- Software controls hardware – without software, a computer is useless.
- Programming requires actual 'hands on' experience.

CHAPTER 4
VARIABLES
AND EXPRESSIONS

Introduction

Conceptually, a variable is like a box with a unique name, into which we can place a value. We may then refer to the box by its name. (Behind the scenes, the box also has a numeric address, which we don't need to be concerned with for the time being.)

Here, we will look at the rules for introducing variables into a program, but the hard part is deciding which variables are required – it depends on practice, experience, and a knowledge of similar examples.

4.1 Numeric Variables

There are two main classes of numeric variable:

- integer (int)
- float (known as 'real' or 'floating-point' in other languages.)

Choose integer for exact, whole-number quantities, e.g:

- the number of students in a class.
- the number of locations in a computer's RAM memory.
- the number of lines on a VDU screen.

Choose float for 'decimal-point' quantities, e.g:

- your height in metres.
- average of several integer numbers.
- mass of an atom.

For real-life problems, you need to be aware of the limitations on the size and accuracy of numeric types. For example, if your computer allocates 16 bits to an integer, this gives you a range of values from aproximately -32000 to +32000. Although the number of customers that a bank has is integer in nature, this range will not accomodate it! Similarly, the number of digits that a float quantity can hold may be as low as 6 ,hence a slight inaccuracy may result when we try to hold 1234.56789.

Though you won't need them often, C provides some additional types:

- long — a large integer, of approximate range -2000 million to +2000 million.
- double — a large float, which typically can hold around 15 digits of precision.
- short — a form of integer, useful when we are dealing with a large quantity of small integers (e.g. in range -100 to +100).

For non-numeric work, e.g. textual data, we can use a 'char' data type, which is described in chapter 9.

4.2 Meaningful Names

As in all programming languages, there are certain rules about how we are allowed to express variable names. In C, the rules are:

- they can contain only letters or digits.
- they must start with a letter.
- they can be as long as we like, but C will only look at the first 8 characters.

Here are some illegal names:

3times, payin£, tax-rate, tax code

Fortunately, C treats the 'underscore' character _ as a letter, so we can use it to improve the readability of names, as in:

exam_mark rather than exammark

Note that upper-case (capitals) are treated as distinct from lower-case, thus:

PAY, pay, Pay are 3 different variables.

Most C programmers stick to lower-case .

Use meaningful names! Your program may be read by other programmers, who need to understand its logic as quickly as possible. Meaningful names will help - e.g:

exam_mark

rather than

em, m, emk.

4.3 Declaring Variables

Along with most modern languages, C insists that you 'introduce' the name of a variable before you use it. These declarations are grouped together near the top of the program. Here is an example:

```
/* some declarations */
#include <stdio.h>
main()
{
    int exam_mark, class_size;
    float height;
    int VDU_size;

    etc
```

(See appendix 1 for further declaration examples).

4.4 Introduction to Expressions

The topic of expressions is a large one in C, but it is important to concentrate on the main features, rather than the mass of detail. A professional C programmer would need to know more than the material presented here, but, for our introductory purposes, a subset will suffice.

Expressions are introduced here via assignment statements, but in fact the expression is allowed in many other contexts – it is an important concept.

4.5 The Assignment Statement

Here are some examples of the simplest form of assignment:

```
/* declare a few variables for the examples  */

    int a,b,c;
    float x,y;

/* now some assignments  */

    a = 1;
    b = 6;
    c = -12345;
    x = 12.34;
    y = 34.5E2;          /* means 34.5 * 10 to power 2 */
    etc
```

'=' should be read as 'becomes', NOT 'equals'.

In C, the right–hand–side of the = is evaluated first, resulting in a single number. This is then assigned to (stored in) the variable on the left–hand–side.
for instance, we are allowed to put –

```
    c = a+b+1;              /* c becomes  8 */
    c = c+1;                /* c becomes  9 */
```

This latter form is particularly common in programming:

c WAS 8. It is now updated to 9.

the general form of an assignment statement is:

variable = expression;

Note the semicolon – we are using statements, and a semicolon terminates every complete statement.

No apologies for repeating:

'=' should be read as 'becomes', NOT 'equals'.

In your very early days of learning C, you might accidentally put:

```
8 = c;
```

The compiler is likely to respond with an error message of the form ' 8 is not an lvalue'. The 'l' in lvalue stands for left, and the compiler is stating that a number is not a suitable place to store a new value, i.e it can't appear on the left of an =.

4.6 Arithmetic Operators

The above examples assumed you would guess what '+' meant, and it does indeed represent addition. It is an example of an arithmetic operator, and the complete set is:

+	addition
–	subtraction
*	multiplication
/	division
%	remainder of integer division

Consider the expression:
    6+4*2
Does it result in 20 or 14 ?

In fact, C follows the algebra convention in performing multiply before add, so the result is 14. The priority of calculation is

- innermost brackets ( ) first – see below.
- * / % next
- + – last.

If all the operators have the same priority, left to right order is used.

Most programming tasks don't involve a rote conversion of algebraic formulae into C assignments, but let's have a look at tricky areas:

Algebra	C
(a) y=mx+c	y=m*x+c;
(b) x=(a-b)(a+b)	x=(a-b)*(a+b);
(c) y=3[(a-b)(a+b)]-x	y=3*((a-b)*(a+b))-x;
(d) $y=1-\frac{2a}{3b}$	y=1-(2*a)/(3*b);
(e) a=-b	a=-b;

In (a) and (b) the * is not assumed, as it is in maths.

In (c), we are forced to use () in every case.

In (d), if we had written 2*a / 3*b , this would have divided by 3 then multiplied by b.

In (e), we have used – for negation.

To complete our look at the arithmetic operators, let us look at integer division, and the '%' remainder (or modulo) operator.
Integers may not be able to cope with very large values, but at least they are guaranteed to be accurate. if we evaluated the integer expression:

```
    3 / 2
```

and we obtained the 'float' answer 1.666667, our accuracy is suspect!

The C solution is to produce an integer result when dividing integers, as in:

```
    a = 3 / 2;          /* a becomes  1     */
    a = 3 / 3;          /* a becomes  1     */
```

Thus, any digits after the decimal point are removed.(known as truncation)

We can find what the integer remainder is by:

```
a = 3 % 2;        /* a becomes  1      */
a = 3 % 3;        /* a becomes  0      */
```

Think this is no use ? Try converting a whole number of cents into the number of dollars and the number of cents left over:

```
dollars = cents / 100;
cents_left = cents % 100;
```

Note that

```
a = 3 % 2.0;
```

would be incorrect as, in C, 2.0 is a float, not an integer.

4.7 Type Conversion in Assignment

If i is int, and f, x are float, what might we expect from:

```
(a)    f = 123;
(b)    i = 12.67;
(c)    i = x;
```

In fact, different languages treat such expressions in different ways. Some would suspect a possible error, and warn you. C accepts all the above assignments!

(a) is not serious. f becomes 123.0, i.e. a float.
(b) is potentially serious. i becomes 12. We have lost some decimal digits.
(c) is like (b), but not as easy to spot, because we have a variable instead of a number.

In short, the right-hand-side is converted to the type of the left-hand-side, even if this results in information being lost.

The Big Picture

We have covered sufficient detail for performing simple numeric assignment statements, but C has over 20 operators, with complicated rules for their use. Fortunately, many of these are used infrequently. The other classes of operator are:

- logical – used to express 'and', 'or', 'not'.
- relational – used to compare values, e.g. 'less than'.
- bitwise – used to access the binary representation of data in RAM.
- assignment '=' – yes, this is itself an operator and can be used in the middle of expressions. In fact, an assignment statement is itself an expression, and can be used in a variety of contexts.
- increment/decrement. Instead of n = n+1 or b = b-1 we may put n++ or b--.

These operators are covered elsewhere.

Additionally, variables can be declared and given a value (initialised) simultaneously, as in:

```
int n = 80;
char c = '+';
```

When the variables are local ('automatic' in C) the initialisation is done each time the function is entered.

Key Points

- Use meaningful names.
- Concentrate on a few simple operators, rather than trying to learn them all.
- Expressions are used in many contexts, not only in assignment statements.

Problems

1. Convert the following mathematical formulae into C assignment statements.

   (a) v = lbh

   (b) y = k(1+x)

   (c) $R_T = \frac{R_1 R_2}{R_1 + R_2}$

2. What are the final values of a,b,c after the following assignment statements?

```
int a,b,c;
a = 1;
b = 2;
c = 3;
a = b+c;
a = a+1;
b = a;
b = a+b*10;
c = b % 10;
```

CHAPTER 5
INPUT - OUTPUT

Introduction

The task of the majority of programs is to read some input data and process it to give some output data (i.e. results). In this chapter, we will look at the simplest form of input-output (I/O for short) involving keyboard for input and screen for output. The use of data files for I/O is described in the 'C Miscellany' chapter, but rest assured that once you know about keyboard/screen I/O, file I/O will present no great difficulty.

5.1 Output - printf

We use the printf() function - formatted print.

In its simplest form, it can display a string of characters enclosed in double-quote marks on the screen, as in:

```
printf("You made an error - try again!\n");
```

note the semicolon - it is a statement, so it needs a terminator.

The quoted string may contain any characters, but certain 'unusual' characters have special significance.

The \n means - 'start a new line'. Behind the scenes, \n is converted to a special character code which controls the screen or printer.

Its use is optional, depending on how you want your output to appear. For example:

```
printf("John\nSmith\n");
```

would produce

```
John
Smith
```

and

```
printf("John ");
print("Smith\n");
```

would produce

```
John Smith
```

However, what we <u>really</u> need is to be able to display the results of calculations – e.g. the values of variables and expressions.

Here is a complete example, which we will extend to include input.

Problem: A lorry is to carry 30 mountain bikes, each of which weigh 18.75 Kg. What is the total load?

Firstly,what type of output is required? In principle, a plain number answers the question, e.g:

562.5

but a more meaningful format is:

--- bikes at --- kg.
Total load is --- kg.

The actual numbers aren't important, because we are discussing <u>layout</u>, and anyway the numbers may change.

In C, we might code this as follows:

```
/* calculate total weight of bikes -  version 1 */
#include <stdio.h>
main(
{
    int num_bikes;
    float one_weight;
    float total_weight;

    num_bikes = 30;      /* later we will read          */
    one_weight = 18.75; /* these values   from keyboard */

    total_weight = num_bikes * one_weight;

    printf("%d bikes at %f kg.\n" , num_bikes, one_weight );
    printf("Total load is %f kg.\n" , total_weight );
}
```

Printf has two forms:

printf("any message");

or

printf("format string" , expression list with commas between items);

The second form is the one for printing the values of variables. What happens is that printf will print every character between "...", but if it encounters a % it will substitute the value of a variable (or expression) from the expression list we supply. This list is processed in left – to – right order. Following the %, we can put some formatting information. For example, 'f' means 'print as a float ', and 'd' means 'print as a decimal integer'.

Consider the statement in the above program:

```
printf("%d bikes at %f kg.\n" , num_bikes, one_weight );
```

The format string is:

```
%d bikes at %f kg.\n
```

Printf works along it from left to right. The first character it encounters is a %, so it looks at the expression list for the first item (num_bikes) and prints its value as a decimal integer. It then continues printing the format string (" bikes at "). The %f tells it to look at the next item in the expression list (one_weight) and print its value as a float. Finally, it prints "kg." followed by a newline character. The output on the screen takes the form:

30 bikes at 18.75000 kg.
Total load is 562.50000 kg.

Here are some more examples of printf:

```
int m, n;
float x,y;
m = 1;
n = 2;
x = 3.5;
y = 4.5;
printf(" %f %d %f %d \n" , x, n, y, m);
printf(" %f %d \n" , (x+12.34)*(y-34.0) , (m-8)*n );
```

Note that expressions can be printed without firstly storing their value in a variable.
Here are some <u>incorrect</u> uses of printf:

```
printf(" %f %f ", x );          /* too few expressions  */
printf(" %f %f ", x, y, x);     /* too many expressions */
printf(" %f %f ",n, x );        /*  n requires  %d      */
```

5.2 Controlling The Format

So far, we have seen %f and %d in format strings, but there are other possibilities. Additionally, we can control how a number is to be displayed – the number of decimal places, etc. Firstly, we will look at the most popular 'conversion specifiers':

%d	–	decimal integer.
%f	–	float.
%e	–	float in 'exponent' form, eg 1.23E+02, where E+02 means ten to power +2.
%c	–	single character.
%s	–	character string.
%x	–	hexadecimal.

Note that, even though we have declared the type of a variable (eg.

float) we must use one of the above conversion specifiers in printf. If we get this wrong, the C system will probably not inform us.

5.3 Controlling The Width

As we have seen, % can be followed by: d,f,e,c,s,x. However, for neat output, we need extra details. For example, we may decide that a float value (say x) is to occupy 7 spaces on the screen, and that only the first 2 decimal places are useful. We specify this by:

```
printf("%7.2f",x);
```

Here, if x doesn't need all 7 positions, printf will put extra spaces at the left to force it to occupy the required 7 positions. This is called 'padding'. Incidentally, the reason why this is a good idea is that output often consists of columns of numbers – if short numbers were to occupy less space than large numbers, the columns would be thrown out of alignment.

Here are some more printf facilities. shown by example:

```
printf("%5d",n);     /* print integer in 5 spaces */
printf("%-5d",n);    /* pad with spaces at right  */
printf("%-7.2f",x);  /* float, padded at right    */
```

5.4 Input – Scanf

Corresponding to printf for output, we have 'scanf' for input. (scan is used in the sense of your eyes scanning along some text, from left to right).

Recall the bike example above. The program we wrote works, but if our data changed, we would need to edit the two assignment statements – not very convenient for us, or for the eventual user, who might not know how to use a text editor. We can arrange for the program to interact with the user, using printf to provide a 'prompt', and using scanf to read the data and store it in the variables :

```
/* calculate total weight of bikes - version 2  */
#include <stdio.h>
main()
{
    int num_bikes;
    float one_weight;
    float total_weight;

    printf("Enter number of bikes, and weight");
    printf(" - space between numbers.\n");
    scanf("%d%f" , &num_bikes , &one_weight );

    total_weight = num_bikes * one_weight;

    printf("%d bikes at %f kg.\n" , num_bikes, one_weight );
    printf("Total load is %f kg.\n" , total_weight );
}
```

When we run the program, the message:

Enter number of bikes, and weight – space between numbers.

appears on the screen, and the user types two numbers. The first number will be stored in num_bikes, and the second in one_weight.

The data could be typed in a variety of ways, e.g:

```
30     18.75
```
or
```
30                 18.75
```
or
```
30
18.75
```

because scanf ignores spaces and newlines between numbers ('white space'). For non–numeric input (e.g. letters of the alphabet), this is not the case.

Scanf has the following form:

scanf("format string" , &variable list, with commas between);

Each % item in the format string must have an associated variable in the variable list. Note that , unlike printf, each variable must be preceded by the '&' character. (This is known as the 'address' operator, and will be described later).

As in printf, we use %d to specify the reading of a decimal integer, and %f to specify float, along with e,c,x,s. The types of variable must agree with the format string. Again, C will not check mistakes such as trying to read into an integer with %f format.

The scanf format string has a wide range of facilities, but here we will look at the possibility of allowing the programmer to control the characters which separate numbers, allowing the user to type, e.g:

30,18.75

Our bikes example was:

```
scanf("%d%f", &num_bikes , &one_weight  );
```

If we wanted the user to separate the values with a comma, we would put

```
scanf("%d,%f", &num_bikes , &one_weight );
```

Here are some <u>incorrect</u> uses of scanf:

```
int m,n;
float x;
scanf("%d%f", &m, &n );     /* n is not float          */
scanf("%d", n);             /* missing  &              */
scanf(n, m);                /* missing format string */
scanf("%d%f  , &n, &x );    /* missing  "              */
```

The Big Picture

- Though we have restricted ourselves to numeric I/O here, most programs also need to handle <u>characters</u>, as in word-processors, spreadsheets, etc. This is treated separately.

- Input errors! With interactive programs, users can make errors when typing data. For example, they may type an 'i' instead of a '1', or a float when an int was expected. In our introductory use of scanf, the program will halt if an input error is detected. This is not ideal however – it is better if the program detects the error and requests the data to be entered again. Scanf has such a facility, and it is described in the C Miscellany chapter.

- Printf and scanf are in fact functions written in C.

Key Points

- C input–output is very flexible and powerful, but it is easy to make errors which will remain undetected until the program runs.

- In printf, ensure that every expression to be printed has a % entry in the format string.

- In scanf, remember the & before every variable, and the % entry in the format string.

Problems

1. What will the following program display on the screen – exactly?

```
#include <stdio.h>
main()
{
    int a,b;
    a=1;
    b=2;
    printf("xx%1dyy%1dzz" ,a,b );
    printf("xx%1dyy%1dzz" , b,a);
    printf("xx%1dyy%1dzz" ,b-a,b+a );
}
```

2. Here is the framework for a program which reads in the dimensions of a rectangle and then prints its area:

```
/* area of rectangle */
   #include <stdio.h>
   main()
   {
      float length,breadth,area;
      scanf("%f%f" , &length,&breadth);
      area = length * breadth;
      printf("%f\n", area);
   }
```

Extend the program so that it

- prints a prompting message telling the user what to type.
- prints its result in the form:

  length is 2.0 cm, breadth is 3.1 cm, area is 6.2 cm sq.

CHAPTER 6
CONDITIONS
AND IF

Introduction

Recall our pseudocode design 'if':

```
if some condition
    do this part when true
else
    do this part when false
endif
```

Here we will see how conditions and 'if' are expressed in C. We will initially look at the basics, leaving the use of assignment in conditions till later.

6.1 Conditions.

Here are the C conditions:

```
==      equal to
!=      not equal to

>       greater than
<       less than

<=      less than or equal to
>=      greater than or equal to
```

They are called 'relational operators'.

We can also combine several conditions using logical operators:

```
&&      and
||      or
!       not
```

Brackets (...) may also be used to group conditions.

Let's look at some conditions in isolation, prior to using them in 'if' statements.

```
int n,m;  /* declare a few vars for examples */
float x,y;

m = 1;
n = 2;
x = 3.67;
y = 0.0;
```

We can now use these variables in conditions, e.g:

```
n < 3                          is true
m == 1                         is true
x >= 4.0                       is false

(n < 3) && (m == 1)            is true
(n < 3) || (m == 1)            is true

(n < 3) && (x >= 4.0)          is false
(n < 3) || (x >= 4.0)          is true

!(m == 1)                      is false
```

These examples illustrate that || && ! work like boolean operators in maths i.e.

- when we 'or' a series of expressions together, we only need one to be true to make the whole expression true

- when we 'and' a series of expressions together, each one must be true to make the whole expression true.

6.2 Equality Testing

Firstly – comparing float numbers. What is the result of the following condition, based on our previous values?

```
x == (4.67-1.0)
```

You might think it is true. it may indeed be true, but in general, we can't be certain. In RAM, the values of float items may have slight inaccuracies, so the condition might be evaluated as:

```
x == 3.670001
```

The solution is to use <= or >= when comparing floats. For example, we might code the above condition as:

```
(x>=(3.67-0.000001) && (x<=3.67+0.000001)
```

We arbitrarily chose 0.000001, but this would depend on the nature of our problem, and the particular computer.

Secondly,the 'equal to ' condition is written == not as = so if you put

```
n = 6
```

instead of

```
n == 6
```

the 'wrong' result will be produced. C won't tell you !
As we will see later, the = has a different meaning in conditions.

6.3 The If Statement

Here is an example of the conversion of a pseudocode design 'if' into C:

```
Pseudocode                    C

if x>y                        if (x>y)
   set a to b                 {
   set c to d                    a = b;
else                             c = d;
   set a to x                 }
   set c to y                 else
endif                         {
                                 a = x;
                                 c = y;
                              }
```

Note that the condition must be enclosed in brackets. and that the else {...} is optional. Strictly, the braces { } can be removed if they only enclose one statement, but it is suggested that you leave them in for now – they do no harm! It is vital to indent the C code. There are a variety of conventions, but it is not important which one you use, as long as you are consistent. Many C systems have a program (called a beautifier or pretty-printer) which will do this for you.

6.4 Nested Ifs

Not surprisingly, C allows an 'if' to enclose other ones. The seldom-used case is when an if is used in the upper 'true' part, as in:

```
if ( x>y)                     /*  A  */
{
   if (n<m)
   {
      printf("%d" , n);
   }
}
else
   ... etc
```

Here, the logic matches what the programmer has shown by the indentation – the else matches with the if at A. But, if we forgot the braces, putting:

```
if ( x>y)
   if (n<m)            /* B */
      printf("%d" , n);
else
   ... etc
```

– the logic doesn't implement what the layout implies, because the C rule for matching else to if comes into force – an else is matched to the nearest if above it. Thus, the else matches the if at B, and the indenting doesn't reflect the interpretation that the C language assumes. Solution – put in { }.

The more common case is when we have nesting in the 'false' lower part, as in:

```
if (exam_mark>=90 )
{
   printf("distinction\n");
}
else if (exam_mark>=75)
{
   printf("credit\n");
}
else if (exam_mark>=40)
{
   printf("pass\n");
}
else
{
   printf("fail\n");
}
```

Though it doesn't match our pseudocode layout (which drifts off to the right of the page) this is the accepted C layout. Obviously, the braces could enclose any number of statements. In the above, we are expressing the situation where there is a list of conditions, one of which will be true, and a list of actions for each case. The optional final 'else' is a 'catchall' if none of the other conditions were met. This pattern is very common.

6.5 Using Else

For beginners, it is tempting to regard 'else' as an optional extra. Consider a program which inputs a number, rejecting it if negative or processing it in some way if positive. We could code it as:

```
scanf("%d",&n);
if (n<0)
   printf("Error! \n");

/* now process it  */
if (n>=0)
{

      ... process it

}
```

It is clearer to put:

```
scanf("%d",&n);
if (n<0)
   printf("Error! \n");
else
{
... process it

}
```

Finally, here is a complete program, using an if statement:

```
   /* program to double a typed number
     or print an error message if negative */
   #include <stdio.h>
   main()
   {
      int number;
      printf("Type an integer:\n");
      scanf("%d", &number);
      if (number < 0)
      {
         printf("error - negative\n");
      }
      else
      {
         printf("double is %d\n" , 2*number);
      }
   }
```

The Big Picture

- There are 3 additional 'bitwise' logical operators – & | ~ which are useful for bit manipulation. These are described in 'C Miscellany'.

- Sometimes, we need to compare a variable against a series of constants (numbers or characters). We can do this with if, as in the problem of converting the numbers 1 to 7 into a day name:

```
scanf("%d",&day_number);
if (day_number==1)
   printf("Sunday");
else if (day_number==2)
   printf("Monday");
...
```

  but the switch statement can be neater. We must use the additional 'break' statement to exit from the selected case to the end of the switch. We have:

```
scanf("%d" , &day_number);
switch (day_number)
{
case 1:
   printf("Sunday");
   break;
case 2:
   printf("Monday");
   break;
case 3:
   printf("Tuesday");
   break;
case 4:
   printf("Wednesday");
   break;
case 5:
   printf("Thursday");
   break;
case 6:
   printf("Friday");
   break;
case 7:
```

```
        printf("Saturday");
        break;
    }
```

- ? : The question-mark is an operator but, like 'if', carries out a selection. The general form is:

  (expression T or F) ? expression T : expression F

  The first expression is evaluated to true or false. Then, one of the following two expressions is selected. Note that the choice is between expressions, not groups of statements: the result is a value. Here is an example: a program is to produce a single-line error summary, of the form

  You have made 0 errors
  You have made 1 error
  You have made 2 errors

  Note the special case of 1 (no 's' is needed). We could do this neatly by:

  ```
  printf("You have made %d error%c\n",count, (count==1) ? ' ':'s');
  ```

Key Points

- In complicated conditions, be careful in your choice of && ||.
- Use == to test for equality.
- Consider using extra brackets (...) in conditions to clarify the meaning of the program.

Problems

1. Write a program which reads in a float number and prints the square of it. An error message should be printed if the number is negative.

2. As Q1, but a warning message should be printed. In any case, square the number.

3. Write a program to read in the dimensions of a rectangle and print its area. An error message should be printed if any dimension is negative.

4. Write a program to read in two integers, and to print them in ascending order.

5. As Q4, but use 3 numbers.

CHAPTER 7
LOOPS:
WHILE AND FOR

Introduction

Frequently, we need to obey the same C statements over and over again, and one way to accomplish this is by setting up a loop (the other way is by recursion). There are a number of loop statements in C, but, following our pseudocode structures, we will concentrate on 'while'. The 'for' statement is also described, because it is convenient for expressing certain types of loops.

7.1 The While Statement

The statement is similar to our pseudocode design one, e.g:

```
Pseudocode                 C

while a<=b do              while (a<=b)
   set a to a+1            {
   set n to n+1               a = a+1;
endwhile                      n = n+1;
                           }
```

As in 'if', brackets ( ) must surround the condition.

The condition is tested at the top of the loop. As long as it is true, the statements in the middle of the loop are obeyed once, and the condition is tested again. As soon as the condition is found to be false, the loop terminates, and the next statement in the program is obeyed. Remember – 'while' means 'as long as'.

Here is a complete program, which reads integers, doubling each one as long as they are positive. The user will type a negative one to stop the program.

```
/* double numbers, stop when negative */
#include <stdio.h>
main()
{
    int number;
    scanf("%d",&number);
    while (number >= 0 )
    {
        printf("%d\n", number *2 );
        scanf("%d" , &number);
    }
    printf("done!  \n");
}
```

There is a more concise way of expressing the program involving the use of scanf in the condition, but we will keep it simple. Note that if the user types a negative number to start with, the program will terminate normally, without attempting to double it.

7.2 The For Statement

The C 'for' is potentially complex, but we will restrain ourselves from its more intricate uses. In programming, 'counting' loops are common, as in:

```
count = 1;
while ( count<=10)
{
    printf("%d\n" , count);
    count = count+1;
}
```

which prints out the integers from 1 to 10 inclusive. We see that initialising, testing, and adding to the counting variable occur in separate statements. The C 'for' allows us to group these three parts together – to make the program easier to follow.

The general form of the C for is:

```
for( start part ; keep going ; bottom part )
{
    optional
    statements
}
```

in which:

'start part' is done once outside the loop.

'keep going' is tested at the top of the loop (as in while)

'bottom part' is done each time through, at the bottom of the loop.

The above 'while' could be expressed with 'for' as:

```
for(count = 1; count <= 10; count = count+1)
{
    printf("%d" , count);
}
```

The complexity can arise because we needn't have <u>any</u> statements enclosed in the loop, and because any of the 3 loop control parts can be omitted. Thus, it is correct C to write:

```
for(;;)
```

which will loop forever.

Here is a reasonable place to recall the increment/decrement operators mentioned earlier.

v++;	is equivalent to	v=v+1;
v--;	is equivalent to	v=v-1;

thus we could write our for as:

```
for(count = 1 ; count<= 10 ; count++)
```

and could count down by:

```
for(v = 10; v>=1 ; v--)
```

To conclude our 'for' discussion, recall the above 1 to 10 loop. What if we wanted to count from 0 to 9 ? Obviously we could put:

```
for(count = 0; count<=9; count++)
```

but equally we could use:

```
for(count = 0; count<10; count++)
```

It doesn't really matter which, but it is important that you understand that they are equivalent – the latter form is widespread in array use, coming later.

The Big Picture

Though 'while' and 'for' are suitable on most occasions, there are some additional facilities.

- Do – while. Here, the statements in the loop are obeyed at least once, and the test comes at the bottom of the loop, as in:

  ```
  n = 0;
  do
  {
      n = n+1;
      printf("%d\n", n); /* prints 1 to 10 */
  }
  while(n<=9);
  ```

  Sometimes this can be more convenient than 'while'.

- Break, continue. In most circumstances, we can collect together the conditions for loop termination, and put them at the top of the loop, e.g:

  ```
  while( (n<=10) && (errors ==0) )
  ```

  Sometimes this is not always possible or convenient, and we may need to use:

  break – the next statement to be obeyed will be the one <u>after</u> the loop.

continue – causes an immediate 'jump' to the condition test.

Here is an example in which the task is to read in 10 numbers, and stop immediately when a negative one is entered. There are a variety of ways to code this – below can be seen the use of 'break':

```
count = 1;
while (count<=10)
{
   scanf("%d",&number);
   if (number<0)
      break;
   count = count+1;
}
```

- Goto. In programming circles, there has been a controversy about the use of 'goto': that its use produced programs that were difficult to read and debug. In retrospect, it seems sensible to reserve its use for certain special situations – typically, breaking out of a lot of nested loops or function calls. Recall that 'break' only takes us out of <u>one</u> loop. We must also introduce a 'label' as destination for the goto. Here is an example in which the program leaps immediately to the end of all the loops:

```
while (...)
{
   while(...)
   {
      while(...)
      {
         ...
         if some error exists
            goto got_error;
      }
   }
}
got_error: printf("serious error!\n");
```

Key Points

- The test for continuing a while loop takes place at the top.
- While can deal with most programming problems – choose this one if in doubt.
- For will be useful when we encounter arrays.

Problems

1. Write a program which firstly reads in two integers (smallest first) , and which then writes out the squares of the integers between (and including) them.

2. Modify Q1 to handle the two numbers in any order.

3. Four programmers produce solutions to this problem:

   "Design a pseudocode algorithm to calculate how many terms of the sum 1 + 2 + 3 + 4 ...
   are needed to exceed 10000."

   Check the following four pseudocode solutions for errors:

A.

```
set term to 1
set sum to 0
while sum <= 10000 do
    set term to term+1
    set sum to sum+1
endwhile
print term on screen
```

B.

```
set term to.0
set sum to 0
    while sum < 10000 do
        set term to term+1
        set sum to sum+term
endwhile
print term on screen
```

C.

```
set term to 0
set sum to 0
while sum<= 10000 do
    set sum to sum+term
    set term to term+1
endwhile
print term on screen
```

D.

```
set term to 0
set sum to 0
while sum <= 10000 do
            set term to term+1
            set sum to sum+term
endwhile
print term on screen
```

4. Write a program to process a series of exam marks, ended by −999(i.e. an unusual mark, called a 'rogue value'). The output is to consist of 3 numbers:

   the average mark
   the number of marks above 40
   the number of marks above 90.

CHAPTER 8
USING AND WRITING FUNCTIONS

Introduction

A function is a self-contained section of a larger program, i.e. a subtask. It is essential to decompose a program into a set of functions, so that its complexity can be managed. Refer to the earlier design chapters for examples of decomposition.

Additionally, C comes with libraries of functions, which we can easily incorporate in our programs. Initially, we will look at using pre-written functions, then look at how we can write our own.

Just as human languages have dialects, so do programming languages. The version of C that has been around for many years is now termed 'old-style' C, and the new standard is ANSI C (American National Standards Institute). The main difference at an introductory level is in declaring functions. This book uses old-style C, which is accepted by any compiler - old or new. However, the slight changes needed to take advantage of the ANSI 'function prototype' are also described.

8.1 C and Libraries

The C language has no built-in functions. Instead it comes with 'libraries' of functions - a library is a collection of related functions. For example, if graphics facilities are provided on a computer system, they will typically be in the form of a graphics library, and in practice, many manufacturers choose C for such tasks.

There are 3 standard libraries on most C systems –

stdio	–	standard i/o library
math	–	square root, sine, cos, etc.
string	–	character – string handling.

When we use a function, we must put the appropriate 'include header' command near the top of our program, e.g:

```
#include <stdio.h>
#include <math.h>
```

Take this on trust for now. The #include directive is covered later.

8.2 Calling Functions

There are two styles of calling (i.e. using) functions:

- as complete statements in themselves, as in:

```
printf("%d" , n);
```

  here, we call the function printf, with two 'arguments' (a character string in quotes and an integer), whose values are passed into the function for it to work on. Printf is a function, written in C.

- or as part of an expression. We will use sqrt (square root) for examples.

```
float x,y;
x = 16.0;
y = sqrt(x);                          /*y becomes 4.0 */
y = sqrt(x+9.0);                      /*y becomes 5.0 */
y = 3.0+sqrt(4.0-sqrt(x)+25.0);       /*y becomes 8.0 */
printf("%f", sqrt(x) );               /*4.0 printed   */
```

  (on most systems, slight numeric inaccuracies will be introduced when floats are stored in RAM.)

We must arrange to do something with the result – e.g. print it out, or assign it to a variable. We shouldn't use it as a statement in its own right, as in this incorrect version:

```
sin(x);
sqrt(16.0);
```

We can find out from system reference manuals what type of arguments a library function requires, and what type of result (if any) it returns. For example, it is specified that sqrt takes a single float as its argument, and returns a float result. (Strictly speaking, the higher-precision 'double' type is specified, but behind the scenes, this is converted to float.)

Even if the function takes no arguments, we must supply brackets, e.g:

```
y = fred();
```

Here is a complete example which prints out square roots of numbers from 1.0 to 10.0

```
/*  square roots -  1.0 to 10.0  */
#include <stdio.h>    /* needed to use printf()       */
#include <math.h>     /* needed to use sqrt()         */

main()   /*  main is in fact a function, hence  ()  */
{
    float x;

    for(x = 1.0 ; x <= 10.0 ; x = x+1.0 )
    {
        printf("%f  %f\n" , x, sqrt(x) );
    }
}
```

and the output would be of the form:

```
1.00000  1.00000
2.00000  1.41421
3.00000  1.73205
   etc, to
10.0000  3.16223
```

8.3 Writing Functions

Any program above say 30 lines will typically be split up into several functions, though the benefits of this approach become more apparent in larger programs. Associated with the concept of a function are the concepts of arguments, local variables, and global variables. To introduce them, we will use an extended analogy:

> Imagine an organisation. 'Main' is the manager, who will call up other workers (functions) to perform subtasks. These workers in turn may call up lower-level workers to do tasks for them, etc. Each worker might need scrap paper for rough work. Rather than requesting paper from the manager, we assume that they are capable of getting their own. This is the equivalent of local variables, which a function can use and create internally. Another approach might be for all the workers to share one large blackboard for rough work – the equivalent of global variables. Now consider one worker's task – perhaps it is to search a filing cabinet for a document. The search process (algorithm) will be the same, irrespective of the name of the document – we need to pass the name of the document to the worker. In C we can pass arguments (data values) into a function for it to make use of.

Here is a complete example:

Assume that we are working on a large program, and one of the minor tasks that must be performed is to draw a line of dashes on the screen, e.g:

```
--------------------          20 dashes
```

We could do this by calling the printf function – the task only takes one call, but let's write a function anyway, to look at the syntax.

```
/* dashes mk 1 */
#include <stdio.h>

void dashes();                    /* a function declaration */

main()
{
   dashes();                /* a call         */
      ...                   /* resumes here */
   etc
}
/************************************/
/* dashes: draws 20 dashes            */
void dashes()                     /* a function definition */
{
   printf("--------------------\n");
}

/****************************/
```

Note:

- The main() function conventionally comes first.

- dashes() doesn't take in any arguments – it always prints 20 – hence the empty brackets ().

- We have used /*******/ comments to emphasize that the function is a separate section of code. Remember that /* */ can contain anything we like.

- When dashes() finishes executing (at its closing }) the program resumes at the point immediately after the point it was called from.

- The keyword 'void' means that the function does not return a result to its caller. (Here, the caller of dashes() is main()).

- For each function, we put a single-line declaration above main. Strictly, you can omit this in some circumstances, but it is worthwhile getting into the habit.

- If you are using an ANSI C compiler, you can take advantage of a 'function prototype', which allows the compiler to make more stringent checks on your program. This is described later – but briefly, the declaration and definition lines in ANSI C would be:

```
void dashes(void);
```

and

```
void dashes(void)
```

Using one statement inside a function is not particularly special, so let's look at an alternative approach to the same problem.

The programmer who wrote dashes() might not have spotted that a single call of printf will do the job – they may have adopted the approach of:

print a "–" 20 times

The mk1 main program will be identical, but the dashes function is coded differently:

```
/* dashes  mk 1 (alternative )  */

void dashes()
{
   int count;
   for( count = 1; count<= 20 ; count = count+1)
   {
      printf("-");
   }
   printf("\n");
}
```

Note where 'count' is declared – it is a local variable, only existing inside the dashes() function. The caller of dashes knows nothing about these locals, and in fact dashes() cannot refer to any locals in main() or other functions. (Note that the C term for local is 'automatic', but the former is common in many other languages.)

Let us now enhance our function. It is now decided that dashes() isn't quite what we need – the program must now produce lines of varying length, as in:

```
- - - - - - - - - - -
- - - - - - - - - - - - - - -
- - - - - - -
- - -
```

etc

Thus, we want to tell dashes() how many to print – we have an 'argument' for it. Here is the program:

```
/* dashes mk 2 */
#include <stdio.h>

void dashes();

main()
{
   int n;
   dashes(20);
   scanf("%d" , &n );
   dashes(n);
   dashes(n+6);
   ...
   etc

}
/*****************************/

void dashes(length)
int length;                        /* type of argument */
{
   int count;
   for(count = 1 ; count <= length ; count++ )
   {
      printf("-");
   }
   printf("\n");
}

/*****************************/
```

Note that the type of the argument(int, float, etc) <u>must</u> be given immediately below the first line of the function.

The programmer who wrote dashes() picked the names 'length' and 'count'. These names are local – only known within dashes, hence there are no problems if other functions have their own similarly-named variables. Local variables lose their value when the function finishes executing.

When the call actually takes place (e.g. dashes(n)) the value of n is transferred into the argument (length) and the function is executed. It is as if there was a ' length = n' taking place behind the scenes. The number of arguments supplied by the caller should match the number declared in the function.

In main() we have shown a variety of argument possibilities – numbers, variables, and expressions. They are calculated before entry to the function and a single value is passed into the argument. Incidentally, we have also used count++ instead of count = count+1.

Additionally, old-style C won't check for type mismatches. If we passed characters instead of an integer, as in:

```
dashes("hello");
```

no warning would be given. In ANSI C, our declaration (i.e function prototype) above main would be:

```
void dashes(int length);
```

and the first two lines of the definition are replaced by the single line:

```
void dashes(int length)
```

The compiler now has advance warning the the dashes function requires an integer expression in brackets, and the above error will be detected. As stated earlier, ANSI C compilers will accept either method of function declaration and definition, but the second form is advisable. Make the machine do the laborious checking!

8.4 Returning Values

In C functions, a return to the caller takes place automatically at the final '}' of the function, but there is also an explicit return statement.

Let us write a function called bigger, which takes in two floats and returns the larger one.

```
/*  returning values   */
#include <stdio.h>
#include <math.h>

float bigger();                         /* declaration */

main()
{
   float x,y,z;
   scanf("%f%f" , &x,&y);

   /* a few example calls  */
   z = bigger(x,y);
   x = bigger(z-2 , sqrt(x+y) );
   printf("%f\n" , bigger(z,10) );
}

/****************************************/
/*   returns bigger of 2 float arguments   */

float bigger(a , b)          /* definition */
float a,b;
{
   if (a>b)
      return a;
   else
      return b;
}
/****************************************/
```

Note:

- We specify the type of result that bigger returns, in both the the declaration and the definition. If you omit it, C won't tell you and your program will give unpredictable results !

- If circumstances require it, we can just put:

  ```
  return;
  ```

  or, we can return any expression e.g:

```
    return sqrt(a/b/c);
```

- Look at the second call of bigger: x = bigger(z−2 , sqrt(x+y)); When the call takes place, the value of z−2 is copied into 'a', and the value of sqrt(x+y) is copied into 'b'. The function then executes using the two copied values.

- A brief /* comment */ has been placed above the function, giving an overview of what it does.

8.5 ANSI Function Prototypes

As you have seen, functions have arguments and results of a variety of types. The difference in the new ANSI C standard is how they are expressed. Rather than stating the rules, sufficient ANSI examples are given which should allow you to write your own.

```
void print_heading(void);
```

print_heading has no result and no arguments.

```
int scale(float x, int n);
```

scale has an int result, and 2 arguments – a float and an int.

```
void sum(float a , float b);
```

sum has no result, and two float inputs.

```
void add_up( int a[] , int size);
```

add_up has no result, and two arguments – an array and an integer.

Remember that these are the declarations, placed in advance (e.g. near the top of the program). The definition of the functions present the same details (without the semicolon), as in:

```
void sum(float a, float b)
{
    printf("%f" , a+b);
}
```

8.6 Global Variables

We have seen the use of arguments to pass values into functions, and 'return' to pass a single result out of functions, but there is an alternative approach using global variables, as in:

```
/*  global example- bad ! */
#include <stdio.h>
#include <math.h>

void bigger();              /* declaration          */

float a,b,answer;           /*global variables      */

main()                      /* print bigger of x,y */
{
   float x,y;
   scanf("%f%f" , &x,&y);
   a = x;
   b = y;
   bigger();
   printf("%f" , answer);
}

/****************************************/
/*  puts  bigger of a,b in answer       */

void bigger()    /* definition          */
{
   if (a>b)
      answer = a;
   else
      answer = b;
}
/****************************************/
```

We have declared a,b and answer above all the functions, making the variables global. (External is the term in C, but global will be familiar to people who use other languages.) This means that they can be used by any function. This may seem simple, in the sense that we have avoided using locals, arguments or return. The arguments have been replaced by assigning x,y to a,b, and the return has been replaced by assigning the result to answer. However, this is regarded as bad programming practice, because:

- Programs with a lot of global variables are hard to understand or debug. Any variable could potentially be altered by any function. In the case of an error, it would be hard to find the incorrect function.

- Arguments are much clearer than the equivalent assignment statements. Additionally, recursion (not covered in this introductory text) is much simpler if arguments are used.

Bearing this in mind, there are certain circumstances where a few global variables are useful – perhaps when a variable (or array) is used by most of the functions in a program. Removing it from the argument list of each function might result in a clearer program. Only experience will enable you to decide.

There is one guideline which covers most cases: when a variable is only used within one function, it should be declared locally.

The Big Picture

- Functions are similar to variables, in that they should be declared before their use. Here we have adopted the approach of declaring all the functions of a program above main(), making them global. Another approach is to declare each function locally in the function which calls it – thus we could have declared dashes within main() rather than above it. The disadvantage of this approach is when a function is called by many other functions – each function must declare it. If not, run-time errors are likely.

- Further function facilities are described in chapter 12.

Key Points

- Try to sub-divide programs into functions.
- Find out if your compiler is ANSI C or not.
- Ensure that the number and type of arguments in the call match those in the definition.
- Before writing a function, check your C library to find out if it (or something similar) exists already.

Problems

1. Write a function called 'smaller', which accepts two integers, and which returns the value of the smaller one.
2. Write a function called 'print_prod' which has two float inputs and no returned result. It prints the sum of the two floats.
3. Making use of dashes(length), write a function called draw_rect with two int arguments - the dimensions of a rectangle - which draws a rectangle on the screen. It returns no result. For example, draw_rect(4,8) gives:

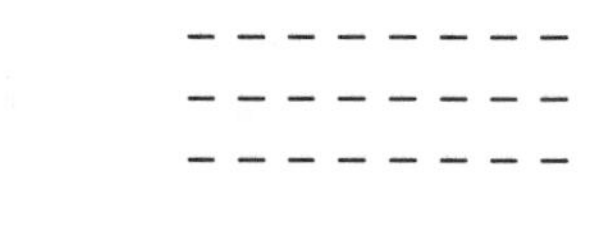

4. Write a function called 'exactly' with two integer arguments, and an integer result. It should return 1 if the two numbers divide exactly, or 0 if they have a remainder. Use the % operator. For example: x = exactly(3,9); sets x to 1.
5. Write a function called 'big3', which returns the biggest of 3 float arguments. Try to make use of the existing 'bigger' function.

CHAPTER 9 CHARACTER VARIABLES

Introduction

Most of the programs in the world don't solve mathematical equations – they manipulate character data. For example – databases, text editors, stock control software, etc. C has facilities to manipulate characters, but there is a lot of detail, and we will postpone much of it until arrays have been covered. Having said that, C is realistic for character manipulation, unlike some other languages.

Here we will look at the manipulation of single-character variables and in a later chapter we will look at character string manipulation (e.g. a person's name) and the available library functions.

9.1 What is a Character ?

Approximately, a character is a symbol on the keyboard, thus:

```
AZab4*- ./
```

is a sequence of 10 different characters (count them – space is included!).

As well as alphabetic, numeric, and punctuation characters, there are others, representing e.g. end-of-line, and special characters used when data is transmitted to other computers. Most computers store a single character in an area of 8 bits, called a byte. If we write down all combinations of 8 bits, from

    00000000
    00000001
        etc
to:
    11111111

we find that there are 256 combinations, which means that (in theory) we could work with 256 different characters.

There is an international standard code for mapping characters to bit patterns (ASCII – American Standard Code For Information Interchange), and most computers (apart from some IBM mainframes) use this. If you consulted the ASCII table, you would find that

A	is represented by		65 (in decimal.)
B	"	"	66
C	"	"	67
	etc		
Z	"	"	90
a	"	"	97
b	"	"	98
c	"	"	99
	etc		
z	"	"	122
0	"	"	48
1	"	"	49
2	"	"	50
	etc		
9	"	"	57
etc			

It is not neccessary to remember that 'A' is represented by 65, but you do need to understand the concept of a unique numeric code for each character.

9.2 Character Variables

They are declared using the keyword 'char', e.g:

```
char fred, initial;
int x;
char jim,sue,l,reply,b;
```

We can assign values, and then test them, as usual:

```
fred = 'a';
jim = 'b';
l = '\n';
```

Note the use of single quotes round a single-character data item.
What we did was to:

put the code for 'a' in fred.
put the code for 'b' in jim.
put the code for newline in l. We have encountered this in printf. The pair \n represents the newline character.

Incidentally, we could have put:

```
fred = 97;
```

but this is harder to follow, and will not work on all computers. In fact, the conversion of 'a' to 97 is done behind the scenes.

Note the important difference between

```
jim = 'b';
jim = b;
```

In the first case, we put the code for the character 'b' in the variable jim, and in the second case, we put the value of the variable b into the variable jim.

Here are some ways of using char variables. Additional comments have been added to the fragments of program – you would not normally comment to this level of detail.

```
/* test if jim holds the character  'z'  */
if (jim == 'z')
   ...
/* loop while b doesn't hold a space (blank) character*/
while (b != ' ')
   ...
/*  test if jim holds a digit  */
if ( (jim >= '0') && (jim <= '9' ) )
   ...
/* test if b holds a letter  */
if ( ( (b>= 'A')&&(b<='Z') )||( (b>='a')&&(b<='z') )  )
   ...
/* convert single digit in b to its int equivalent  */
x = b - '0';
```

The above common bits of program should be understandable if you remember that characters are represented internally by numbers. Thus, > means 'after', and < means 'before'.

9.3 Character Example

In chapter 8, we developed a function to draw a line of dashes on the screen, e.g:

```
dashes(6);
```

produced

```
------
```

Let us add a second argument to allow the user of the function to control the actual character that is printed, as well as the number of characters, i.e. to allow the printing of e.g:

*** or //////

The function to perform this is:

```
void line_of_chars(length, anychar)
int length;
char anychar;
{
    int count;
    for (count=1; count<=length; count++ )
    {
        printf("%c" , anychar);
    }
    printf("\n");
}
```

We may call it by e.g:

```
line_of_chars(3,'*');
line_of_chars(6,'/');
```

In the above, we have introduced %c to specify the printing of a single character. Recall that we have used %d and %f in the past.

The ANSI C function prototype would be:

```
void line_of_chars(int length , char anychar);
```

9.4 Character I/O

- To output the single character in b, we can put:

  ```
  printf("%c", b);
  ```

- To input a character from the keyboard into b , you can use:

  ```
  scanf("%c" , &b);
  ```

  Spaces and the end-of-line character will not be ignored.

As you will be aware, most computers allow you to correct a typed input line (e.g. by backspacing, etc) before entering it (by pressing the return or end-of-line key). This means that the characters will not reach scanf until return is pressed. Behind the scenes, each character is stored in an area of RAM called a 'line buffer' – they are not sent immediately to scanf. Eventually, the end-of-line key is pressed, and then scanf processes the characters. For example, if our input consisted of a character followed by an integer (e.g. r 43) we could read it in several ways. The most obvious approach is to read both items together, as in:

```
scanf("%c%d" , &any_char , &number );
```

but we could process them by:

```
scanf("%c" , &any_char );
    ...
/* lots of C code  */
    ...
scanf("%d" , &number );
```

The nature of the problem determines the best approach.

9.5 Efficient I/O

C has become known as a language in which it is possible to write programs that run quickly. If you are trying to produce software which does a lot of character I/O (as many programs do) , bear in mind that statements that are executed frequently have a greater overall effect on speed than those which execute once or twice. Printf and scanf will get a lot of use in character-processing programs, so C provides some more efficient alternatives , called getchar and putchar. Getchar returns a result, so we must use it as part of a statement, rather than as a complete statement in itself, e.g:

```
b = getchar();        /*read next char into b  */

putchar(b);           /*print char in b        */

putchar('X');         /*print an 'X'           */
```

Thus

b = getchar()	is equivalent to	scanf("%c" , &b)
putchar(b)	is equivalent to	printf("%c" , b)

Getchar and putchar are used in many C programs, and later we will look at a particular style of use in 'while' loops. Incidentally, although getchar and putchar look like functions, they are in fact macros, handled by the preprocessor.

9.6 The ctype Library

Earlier, we looked at how characters could be classified as letters or digits. This operation is very common, so a "character-type" library exists, with such functions as:

isupper(c)	true if upper case
islower(c)	true if lower case
isdigit(c)	true if a single digit.

Where c is a character variable, or a character in ' '.

You must put:

```
#include <ctype.h>
```

at the top of your program, and you may then use the functions, as in:

```
getchar(b);
if ( isdigit(b) )
    ...
```

As with getchar, we use them as functions, but behind the scenes they are macros.

The Big Picture

- If you are familiar with the manipulation of variable-length character strings in other languages, C char variables will disappoint you. Consult chapter 13 for this facility.

Key Points

- A character variable can only hold a single character.

- Characters are enclosed in single quotes. The use of double quotes is likely to be accepted by your C compiler, but incorrect results will occur.

- The > < operators can be used to compare characters.

- The ctype library should be used when appropriate – don't re-invent the wheel!

Problems

1. Write a program to read in a line of text, ended by \n, and print its length. Does it work for a zero-length line?

2. Assuming that a sentence has a single space between each word and ends with a full stop, write a program which reads in a sentence and calculates the average word length.

3. Making use of the 'line_of_chars' function, produce the pseudocode design of a program which inputs the dimensions of a rectangle and draws a box, as in:

   ```
   ******
   *    *
   *    *          ( 6 by 4)
   ******
   ```

   Try to split the program into several functions.

4. Write a program which reads in lines of the form:

   3*4+2;
   1*2*3+8*37;

   and which prints out the answer. Assume that we can only use + and *, and that the line is ended by a semicolon. To simplify the task somewhat, the calculations are to be performed in strictly left-to-right order, rather than doing * before +.

CHAPTER 10
AN INTRODUCTION TO ARRAYS

Introduction

Frequently, the data we need to manipulate is in the form of a table – for example a list of names or numbers. There are several possibilities for storing them in RAM: perhaps the easiest to understand is the array. If you have studied matrices in maths, you will find the concept familiar.

Consider this problem – input 3 numbers, and print them out in reverse order. The solution is very simple, consisting mainly of:

```
scanf("%d%d%d", &a,&b,&c);
printf("%d %d %d", c,b,a);
```

What if we wanted to reverse 1000 numbers? With what you know up to now, you would use the same basic approach, but with 1000 variables, e.g:

```
scanf("%d%d%d%d etc......  " , &aa,&ab,&ac,&ad, ...);
```

Obviously this is a ridiculous approach.

In fact, we would usually tackle this problem using an array.

An analogy could be made to a prison, consisting of cells (each containing one prisoner). The governor could give each cell a name (eg- Dunroamin, The Larches, South Fork ...) and could then issue commands to warders such as ' put the new prisoner in Dunroamin', or 'swap over the prisoners in The Larches and South Fork', but for certain types of commands, it is more convenient to refer to each cell by a number, known as a subscript in C. Commands to the warders now take the form 'put prisoner in cell 6', or, using a variable:

```
set n to 6
put prisoner in cell n
```

So far, no great advantages. But what about a command to release the prisoners in every cell? This would be very tedious if each cell had a name, but our array of numbered cells would allow commands of the form:

```
for(n = 0 ;n<100 ; n++ );
    {
        release prisoner in cell n
    }
```

10.1 One – dimensional Arrays

In C, we can declare arrays, and give them meaningful names. We can then select individual elements by an integer subscript. The array exists in RAM, and can be accessed very quickly (e.g. 1 microsecond per element).
In our prison analogy, we would call the array 'cell', and we could then refer to e.g:

```
cell[6]
cell[n]
cell[n+2]
etc.
```

Square brackets must surround the subscript.

We declare arrays at the same place in the program as other variables, e.g:

```
int x;
int a[4] , b[5];
float age[70];
int cell[100];
char myname[5]
```

When we declare the array, we specify the type of each element and the number of elements. The first element has a zero subscript. Thus, we have declared an array called 'a', with elements a[0] , a[1] , a[2] , a[3]

Pictorially, we can represent it as:

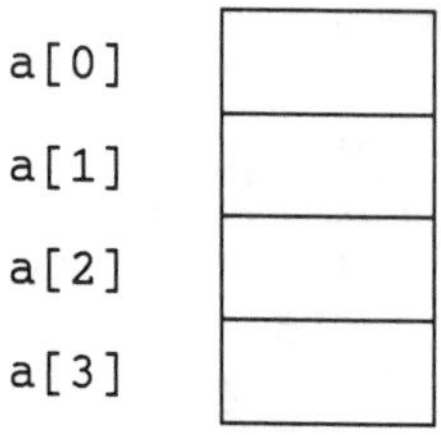

a[0]	
a[1]	
a[2]	
a[3]	

As you can see, this is a single column of 'boxes', each of which can hold a number. For this reason, it is called a 'one-dimensional' array. Later, we will see that a two-dimensional array is a 'grid' of boxes, like a chess board. Appendix 1 has an additional example.

You may be familiar with arrays in other languages - if so you will be aware that the above numbering system is slightly different, in that subscripts always begin at zero.

It is not possible to perform operations on a whole array with one statement - we would have to write functions to do this - but individual elements are just like variables, and can be manipulated in the same way. Thus, because we can write statements of the form:

```
n = g * (f-4);
printf("%d" , 2 * n);
```

we can also put:

```
a[2] = b[x-8] * (a[0] - 4);
printf("%d" , 2*a[x*x+3]);
```

Subscripts in [] can be expressions.

10.2 Range of Subscripts

Consider

```
int a[4];
```

The programmer intends (with the best will in the world) to only use subscripts for 'a' in the range 0 to 3. but the programmer could get it wrong. For example, statements such as:

```
scanf("%d",&n);        /* read n from keyboard */
x = a[n];
```

can give a wrong result if '4' is typed. Some languages will check this and halt the program, but C won't. In general this is true of many C constructs – C won't check! The safe version of the above would have an 'if' to check n and prevent execution of the second statement in certain cases. Additionally, if your program has a bug, one of the areas to check is subscripts. For example, a common error is to think that

```
int a[4];
```

allows you to use 1 to 4 as subscripts.

10.3 Reversing Numbers

Here is a solution:

```
/* reversing a sequence of 1000 numbers Mk 1  */
#include <stdio.h>
main()
{
    int n;
    int data[1000];

    for(n = 0; n<1000; n++)
    {
        /* read number into n'th element  */
        scanf("%d" , &data[n]);
    }
    for( n = 999; n>=0; n--)
    {
        /* print n'th element on a new line */
        printf("%d\n" , data[n] );
    }
}
```

Many array problems involve the above pattern of doing the same operation on each element, thus the above 'for' loop is very common. Only the part between the 'for' loop braces {   } will change. Assuming that data has been read into the array, here is how we could add up all the elements:

```
sum = 0;
for(n = 0; n <1000; n++)
{
    sum = sum + data[n];
}
```

Check the conditions in the 'for'. The variable n takes the value 0 to 999, which is correct – there are 1000 elements. This style of use (<1000 rather than <=999) is favoured. Whilst on the topic of array sizes, a frequent maintenance task is to alter the size from time to time. The above reversing program mentions 1000 (or 999) 3 times, and later we will see how the C '#define' facility would allow us to state the size once only, making it easy to amend.

10.4 Searching

Frequently, we need to search an array for a particular value. When the contents of the array are in a particular order (e.g. ascending), we might consider an algorithm which looks at the middle element, and then decides which half of the data to examine – rather in the way one might search a dictionary. However, we will assume that the values in the array have no pattern to them, and we will step through them one at a time, stopping when we find the required one. This is analogous to the compact disc search in the earlier design chapter. Note that, when searching there are two conditions: we keep looking as long as we haven't found the value, and as long as we haven't reached the end of the array.

Here is the complete program – because we have not yet covered arrays as arguments , it has not been split into functions. The program reads in 20 numbers, then asks the user to type a number. It is reported as not found, or found at a particular position. Incidentally, when we study the C preprocessor we will see an alternative to the explicit use of 0 and 1 to represent 'yes' and 'no' in the 'found' variable.

```
/* search array sequentially */
#include <stdio.h>
main()
{
   int data[20];
   int place;
   int wanted,found;

   /* read in the data  */

   for(place = 1; place<20; n++)
   {
      printf("type a number:\n");
      scanf("%d", &data[place] );
   }
   /* request the data value to search for */

   printf("Which number to find?\n");
   scanf("%d" , &wanted);

   /* do the search */

   found = 0;        /* 0 means  'not yet' */
   place = 0;
   while ( (place <20) && ( found = 0 ) )
   {
      if ( data[place] == wanted )
         found = 1;        /* 1 means 'yes' */
      else
         place++;
   }
   if (found == 0)
      printf(" %d was not found \n" , wanted );
   else
      printf("%d  at position %d \n",wanted, place);
}
```

Note the the output is of the form:

```
235  at position 13
```

In most search applications, is is vital that we know the position of the result – we may use it modify the value, or as a subscript for a second array.

10.5 Finding the Largest

Our task is to examine the array elements to find the one containing the largest. Again, it is important to find the position of the largest.
The algorithm assumes that the first one is the largest, then examines the rest of the elements in turn. A 'largest place so far' variable is used, which is reset if need be.

```
/* largest in an array */
#include <stdio.h>
main()
{
    int data[20];
    int place;
    int large_place;

    /* read 20 values into data[], as in 10.4 */

    /* find largest */
    large_place = 0      /* assume first is largest */
    for(place = 1; place<20; place++)
    {
        if ( data[place]>data[large_place] )
            large_place = place;
    }
    printf("largest is %d \n" , data[large_place] );
    printf("and its position is %d \n" , large_place);
}
```

The output is of the form:

```
largest is 2365
and its position is 13
```

10.6 Arrays as Arguments

Recall our number reversing problem: thinking about this at a design level, we might have come up with:

read data into array
print data backwards

then, getting closer to C, we might come up with

read_data()
print_data()

We could declare the array globally at the top of the program, but this is not always desirable. A better alternative might be to pass the array into each function as an argument.

There is a convention about passing arrays – we pass the name of the array, and its size. Thus, the size comes in to the function as an argument in (..) not as a global or #defined item. This makes it possible to write functions which work on different sizes of arrays – a very important feature (not available in some other languages).
Our solution is now:

```
/* reversing a sequence of 1000 numbers Mk 2 */
#include <stdio.h>
void print_data();        /* declarations */
void read_data();
main()
{
    int data[1000];
    read_data(data, 1000);
    print_data(data, 1000);
}

/*****************************************/

void read_data(a,anysize)
int a[];
int anysize;
{
    int n;
    for(n = 0; n<anysize; n++)
    {
        /* read number into n'th element */
        scanf("%d" , &a[n]);
    }
}
```

```
/****************************************/

void print_data(a,anysize)
int a[];
int anysize;
{
    int n;
    for( n = anysize-1; n>=0; n--)
    {
        /* print each one on a new line */
        printf("%d\n" , a[n] );
    }
}
```

Incidentally, the ANSI function prototype would be e.g:

```
void print_data(int a[] , int anysize);
```

Note:

- n is a conventional local variable.
- As before, we must specify the type of each argument. For a one-dimensional array, we just need to put [ ]. No size is specified at this stage.
- In common with other arguments, we have free choice of names for array arguments. 'a' was chosen, but any name would do.
- The size of the array is usually passed as an additional argument.
- In C, arguments are passed 'by value', but for arrays, the value that is passed is the address of the first element in memory. This enables the function to locate the first element and hence the whole of the array. In the above program, there is only <u>one</u> array, known as 'data' in main, and as 'a' in the other functions. We simply give each function its whereabouts in RAM. The function can modify the array if required.

Here is another example: let us write a function to add up the elements of an array – you have seen the logic of it before, but not wrapped up as a function. Because the function produces a single integer as an answer, we can use 'return' to pass the result back to the calling program We assume that values have already been stored in the array.

```
/* this function sums 'size' elements
 of the int array a                    */
int sum_of(a,size)
int a[];
int size;
{
    int n, sum;
    sum = 0;
    for( n = 0; n<size; n++)
    {
        sum = sum + a[n];
    }
    return sum;
}
```

Let us declare a few arrays, to show the capability of this simple function:

```
int a[800];
int salary[100];
int b[2];
int x,y;
```

Assuming that we arrange to put values in these arrays, we could use our function in these ways:

```
x = sum_of(a,800);
x = sum_of(salary,100);
x = sum_of(salary,10); /* sum of first 10 elements  */
y = sum_of(salary,10) + sum_of(b,2);
printf("%d" , sum_of(b,2) );
```

Certain features of C have been purposely ignored in this chapter – for example , what if we wanted to extend our sum function to also return the smallest number in the array? In C, 'return' can only be used to pass back a single value, and additional techniques are needed in this case. In fact, scanf is a function that passes back several values, so it is apparent that such functions <u>can</u> be written. This facility is explained in chapter 11.

Though arguments (sometimes called parameters) are initially a difficult topic, they are difficult in all languages and are widely used by all professional programmers. In C we can write functions to handle arrays of any size, and because strings are regarded as arrays of characters, we can write string-handling functions – or use the existing library of routines.

The Big Picture

- C has the concept of a pointer, i.e. a variable which holds the whereabouts (the address) of an item. For example, in Appendix 1, the array a[ ] is stored at address 9005 onwards. We could arrange for a totally separate variable (say pa) to point to the array by storing 9005 in it. There are now two ways to refer to element number 2: as a[2] , or pa+2.

Key Points

- Array elements exist in RAM and can be manipulated just like other variables.

- An individual element is selected by a subscript – an expression in [ ]. Recall that expressions include numbers, variables, and calculations.

- To perform the same operation on each element of an array, we often use a 'for' to step through the elements.

Problems

1. These problems are based on 12 integers – the rainfall data for each month of a year. You will need to invent suitable numbers, and read them into an array at the start of your program. An initial decision is whether to use:

```
int rainfall[12];
```

which allows you to refer to the elements as rainfall[0] to rainfall[11], or to use:

```
int rainfall[13];
```

which allows rainfall[1] to rainfall[12]. In this case , element zero will be unused.

a). Write a program which reads the data into an array, then finds the largest rainfall figure.

b). Extend a). so that it prints the month number as well.

c). Extend b). so that it finds the average rainfall per month.

2. Using an array of char, write a program which inputs a series of characters ended by a newline (\n) and which prints them vertically. Thus:

   fred

   becomes

   f
   r
   e
   d

   Assume there is always less than 20 characters.

3. Write a program which reads the rainfall data into an array, and then prints a simple 'sideways' histogram, of the form:

```
month     rain
  1        15  !***************
  2        18  !******************
  3        10  !**********
      etc
```

Assume that no rainfall exceeds 60.

CHAPTER 11
The C PREPROCESSOR

Introduction

Though we talk about compiling a C program as if it were one step, behind the scenes there are two parts – preprocessing and compilation. Compilation proper consists of error checking and the production of machine code, whereas preprocessing is a kind of automatic editing that is performed on the text of the program prior to compilation. It is controlled by directives, indicated by '#'. Here we will look at the most useful directives one by one.

11.1 #define

This is one of the simplest directives, used to make programs more readable and easier to amend. Here is an example: assume we are writing a program which makes frequent use of pi (3.14159 approx.). For example:

```
x = 3.14159;
    ...
circ = 2.0*3.1549*r;
```

The second line is incorrect – digits have become transposed. To avoid such errors we could create a variable called pi and give it the correct value, but pi isn't really a variable – we never want to change its value. The C style is to use #define, as in:

```
#include <stdio.h>
#define PI 3.14159
main()
{
   float x,r,circ;
   ...
x = PI;
circ = 2.0*PI*r;
   ... etc
```

The #define is a directive (an instruction) to the preprocessor, telling it to replace any occurrence of the string 'PI' by '3.14159'. The resulting modified program is then compiled. In the above, the text that is eventually compiled is:

```
x = 3.14159;
circ = 2.0*3.14159*r;
```

Here, we are following the C convention of using capitals for defined items. It is considered good programming practice to use #define, rather than writing numbers directly in the program. For example, using the number 80 in a program is meaningless, but if we put:

```
#define  SCREENWIDTH  80
   ...
if ( n>SCREENWIDTH )
   ...
```

we have a more readable program. Avoid 'magic' numbers!

The preprocessor does <u>no</u> error checks. If we incorrectly put:

```
PI = 8.6;
```

it would be correctly preprocessed to:

```
3.14159 = 8.6;
```

and the compiler would produce an error message of the form:

"3.14159 not an lvalue – can't be used on left of = "

Thus, the error message doesn't mention PI – it refers to the text of the line after it has been preprocessed. This is not ideal, but at least it won't allow the program to compile and run!

A common requirement in program maintenance is to change the size of an array, to allow it to accomodate more data. We can allow for this in advance by using #define for the size. As an example, consider the reversing program in chapter 10 – the size is mentioned several times as an actual number (e.g 1000 or 999). However, if we put:

```
/* reversing a sequence of  numbers- e.g of #define  */
#include <stdio.h>
#define SIZE 1000
   main()
   {
      int n;
      int data[SIZE];

      for(n = 0; n<SIZE; n++)
      {
         /* read into n'th element */
         scanf("%d" , &data[n]);
      }

      for( n = SIZE-1; n>=0; n--)
      {
         /* print each one on a new line */
         printf("%d\n" , data[n] );
      }
   }
```

Note that instead of 999 we have put SIZE – 1 which the pre-processor converts to 1000 – 1 prior to compilation.
If we want to change the amount of data, all we do is change the #define to e.g:

```
   #define SIZE 2000
```

There is no restriction on the number of #defines in a program. However, they are not C statements, and should not be indented or followed by semicolons.

11.2 #define macro

A rather more difficult facility of #define is that of macro-definition. A macro is a form of shorthand, similar in nature to our previous simple use, but more powerful. One string is replaced by another, but, in addition, arguments can be substituted in the string. As an example, we might be working on a program which involved cubing variables:

```
v = a*a*a;
y = fred*fred*fred;
```

We could write a function to do this, but the overhead of function calling (transferring arguments, saving the return address etc) would be significant for such a quick calculation. Instead, we could define it as a macro:

```
#define CUBE(x)  (x*x*x)
```

The difference from our earlier #define is the brackets, indicating a macro. 'x' is the argument, allowing us to use the macro with any variable name, not only x. If we put:

```
v = CUBE(a);
y = CUBE(fred);
```

the preprocessor would substitute a and fred for x, as it 'expands' the macro. The resulting code would be:

```
v = a*a*a;
y = fred*fred*fred;
```

It is important not to confuse this with arguments and functions at run-time. #define, with macros or not, is a purely textual operation happening before compilation.

The above CUBE works for variables and numbers, but not expressions. If we put:

```
v = CUBE(n+3);
```

the resulting code would be:

```
v = n+3*n+3*n+3;
```

in which all the 3*n calculations would be done first. A better version is:

```
#define CUBE(x)    ((x)*(x)*(x))
```

which would produce:

```
v = (n+3)*(n+3)*(n+3);
```

The outer brackets are always needed, and the inner brackets force n+3 to be evaluated first.

The 'functions' getchar() and putchar() are in fact macros on most systems, which are converted into calls of an I/O function with complicated arguments.

11.3 #include

As you have seen, #include is usually placed near the top of a program. It is followed by a file name, as in:

```
#include <stdio.h>
#include <math.h>
#include "myfile.h"
```

The use of < > signifies a 'system' file, whereas " " signifies a file (typically) in one of your personal directories.

The action of #include is basically simple – it is the style of use that is tricky. Here is an introductory example – not typical, but simple to follow:

We have two files; the first is called demo.c, containing:

```
/* demo.c*/
#include "vars.c"
main()
{
    a = 4;
    b = 2;
    a =a+b;
}
```

The file vars.c contains:

```
/* vars.c */
int a;
int b;
```

The action of #include is as follows: we compile demo.c, as usual. When the compiler reaches the #include line, it switches to the specified file (vars.c here). At the end of this file, it continues to compile the original demo.c file. Included files can also contain #include.

Thus, the compiler processes the following C code:

```
/* demo.c*/
/* vars.c */
int a;
int b;
main()
{
   a = 4;
   b = 2;
   a = a+b;
}
```

Having looked at a simple example, let us look at the most common pattern of use – for 'headers'. Imagine we have written two functions for other programmers to use, which are declared at the top of the program as:

```
float biggest();
float smallest();
```

(In ANSI C, we would also add details about the types of arguments.) If other programmers wanted to use the functions, we could give them the source code of the functions, together with the above two declaration lines, but the C approach is to use compiled versions, rather than source code. Here is what would take place: firstly, we would create a file called, say, "statistics.h" and put the above two declaration lines in it. Secondly, we would compile the functions by themselves and put the machine code (or object code) in a file called "statistics.o". (The technique of doing this depends on your C system.) These two files would then be made available to other programmers, who could then incorporate our functions by putting:

```
#include "statistics.h"
```

at the top of their program, and by issuing a system command to 'link' to the "statistics.o" file during compilation. In this manner, the actual source code of the functions and declarations is not needed.

In general, files ending in ".h" are header files, containing details of function argument and return types.

11.4 #ifdef – #endif

This directive instructs the compiler to ignore certain lines of the program. For example, when debugging a program, a popular approach is to put printf statements at the entry to most functions, as in:

```
void sort(x)
int x;
{
   printf("In sort, argument is %d \n" , x );
   ... etc
}
```

When most of the bugs have been found, we might wish to dispose of this additional 'trace' output. It would be possible to do this with a text editor, or by commenting them out with /* */, but #ifdef could be used as follows:

```
#define  TRACING
/* lots of functions... etc */
void sort(x)
int x;
{
#ifdef TRACING
   printf("In sort, argument is %d \n" , x );
#endif
   ... etc
}
```

The action of #ifdef is to check if the mentioned item has been #defined – here it has, so all the lines between #ifdef and #endif are compiled. If we deleted the #define directive, the lines between #ifdef and #endif would be ignored by the compiler.

11.5 Defining Booleans

Here we show a practical application of the preprocessor – the creation of 'boolean' values. Boolean algebra was invented by George Boole, and deals with true/false values. In a sense, we have encountered them earlier in C, when such statements as:

```
if (x == 3)
    printf("x is 3");
else
    printf("x is not 3");
```

Here, x == 3 is evaluated , resulting in 'true' or 'false'.

Imagine that we want to write a function called 'valid_age' with one argument as input – say the age of a person, as an integer. The function will tell us whether the age is in the range 16 to 65. A true/false result will be returned, which can be tested, as in:

```
if( valid_age(64) )
```

or

```
while (  valid_age(my_age) )
```

In the body of the function, we will need to pass back the result, e.g:

```
return (some true value)
```

Other languages have the keywords 'true' and 'false' built in , so we might put:

```
return (true);
```

but in C, the programmer has to be aware that the concept of FALSE is represented by 0, and any other value (eg – 9, 33, 1, –76) is treated as TRUE. When we set something to true, we use 1.

false	0	
true	1	(or any other non–zero value).

Our required function is:

```
int valid_age(age)
int age;
{
   if (  (age >=16) && (age<=65) )
      return( 1);        /* i.e  true */
   else
      return( 0);        /* i.e false */
}
```

and we call the function as shown above.

When we looked at #define earlier, we suggested avoiding 'magic numbers', by defining them as names. At the top of the program, we could put:

```
   #define TRUE 1
   #define FALSE 0
   #define BOOLEAN int
```

and our function could then be made more understandable:

```
BOOLEAN valid_age(age)
int age;
{
   if( (age>=16)&&(age<=65)  )
      return (TRUE);
   else
      return (FALSE);
}
```

but behind the scenes, 0/1 is still used.

Note that if, by accident, you wrote
`return(age);` instead of `return(TRUE);`

our call of the form:

```
   if( valid_age(80) )
      ...
```

will end up evaluating

```
if( 80 )
```

and will find a true value. In 'strongly-typed' languages like Pascal, Modula 2, and Ada, the programmer could specify that a variable like 'age' can only hold numeric values, and that a variable such as, e.g. 'married' can only hold true/false values. In such languages, if we put such statements as

```
age = TRUE;
married = 65;
married = age;
```

we would get a compilation error. In C the program would be accepted.

Key Points

- Use #define to replace meaningless items by meaningful names. 'Initialising' or 'starting' numbers like 0, 1 are usually left as they are.
- You will make use of macros (e.g. getchar()) but will rarely need to write your own.
- try to make programs readable and easy to change.

Problems

1. Examine the contents of your <stdio.h> and <math.h> files.
2. Write a program which uses sqrt, but omit the #include <math.h>. Does it compile on your system? If so, are the results correct?
3. Use #define to allow the programmer to use ENDIF and ENDWHILE in a program, instead of braces.
4. Define a macro called INTPRINT(X) which does the equivalent of printf("%d" , x). It should work for any expression, not just x.

5. Assume that you are working on a program which will eventually run on two types of hardware – one has an 80 character screen width, and the other has a 132 character screen. Obviously we would #define them, but show how #ifdef could be used to make the process simpler.

CHAPTER 12 FURTHER ARRAYS AND FUNCTIONS

Introduction

Previously we have looked at one-dimensional arrays, which can be imagined as a single column (or row, depending on how we choose to draw them) of items. Here we advance to two-dimensional arrays, which can be imagined as a 'grid' of variables. Each element now needs two subscripts to identify it. In addition, we look at pointers as applied to passing back several values from a function.

12.1 Declaring and Accessing

Arrays in C can have any number of dimensions, but most programs only go up as far as 2. Although computers know nothing about the concepts of horizontal and vertical, it is useful to imagine such arrays as:

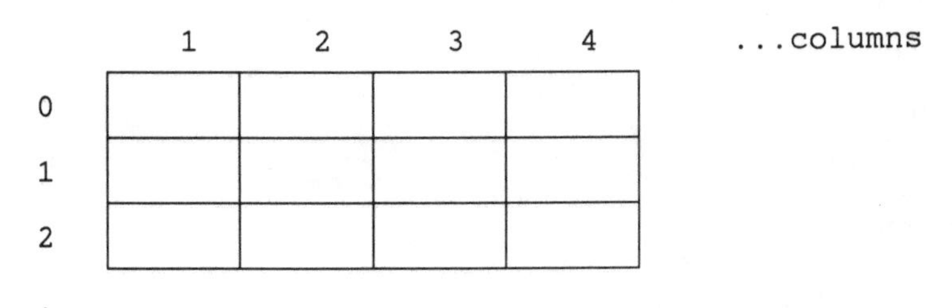

There are 4 columns and 3 rows – recall that we count from zero in C.

When we declare the array, we need to supply the two sizes, and when we want to access one element, we must supply 2 subscripts.

The above array (assuming that it is to hold integers) could be declared by:

```
int a[3] [4]; /* [number of rows] [number of columns] */
```

and we could put a value in the bottom right element by:

```
a[2][3] = 2001;
```

Often, we may want to perform the same operation on each element of the array, and a nested 'for' pattern can be used, e.g:

```
for(row = 0; row<3; row++)
{
    for(col = 0; col<4; col++)
    {
        a[row][col] = 0;
    }
}
```

Here, we have put 0 in each element. The order of accessing elements in this task is not vital, and we chose to work across a row, then move down to the next row. However this way is useful, as it matches the way printers move across paper – across a row rather than down a column. The integer variables row and col (your choice of name) thus take the succession of values

row	col
0	0
0	1
0	2
0	3
1	0
1	1
1	2
etc, to	
2	3

Here is another example, showing how an array could be used in a noughts and crosses game program. A complete program would be rather long, with input validation and win detection, but we will look at a few fragments of code. Because the board is likely to be used by many functions (and because there is only one board) we might choose to make the array global, rather than pass it as an argument (shown later).

We could represent the blank board by a 3 by 3 array of char, initialised to dots, e.g:

```
. . .
. . .
. . .
```

We might declare

```
int row,col;
char board[3][3];          /* 0  1  2  */
```

and clear the board by our familiar nested 'for' pattern:

```
for(row = 0; row<3; row++)
   for(col = 0; col<3; col++)
      board[row][col] = '.';
```

We will need to ask the player to specify where their next move is to be – the program will know whether it is a O or X. We will omit a check for the range 0f 0 to 2, but will check an attempt to go in a square that is not a '.'.

```
printf("Type row and column number - 0 1 2 \n");
scanf("%d %d", &row, &col );

if (board[row][col] != '.' )
   printf("Cheat! - Used already!\n");
else
   board[row][col] = 'X';
```

For a high – quality game, we might use functions from a graphics library (possibly written in C) to control the screen and cursor.

12.2 2 – Dimensional Arguments

Much play was made earlier about how functions could be used to manipulate arrays of any size. This also enables 1 – dimensional arrays of char to represent strings, as detailed in chapter 13.

Unfortunately, this does not apply to multi-dimensional arrays, and a slightly different approach is needed.

Let us write a function that initialises every element of a 2-dimensional array to a particular value (e.g. 0, as above). Here is the code:

```
void init_2d(x,num_of_rows, aconstant)
int x[] [4];          /* must fix number of cols here  */
int num_of_rows;
int aconstant;
{
    int row,col;
    for(row = 0; row<num_of_rows; row++)
        for( col = 0; col<4; col++)
            x[row][col] = aconstant;
}
```

Let us assume that these arrays are declared in the main program:

```
int a[3][4];
int b[80][4]
int c[80][5];
```

We could call our function, by, e.g:

```
init_2d(a,3,0);         /* set all  a  to  0 */
init_2d(b,80,-1);       /* set all  b  to -1 */
```

but should not put

```
init_2d(c,80,-1);
```

because the other dimension of c is not 4, and we specified 4 in the function. Thus we have a certain amount of freedom – our function can accept an array of a different number of rows, but the number of columns (or the length of a row, which is another way of looking at it) must be fixed.

12.3 Arrays of Arrays

If we wanted to store an array of (say) 200 persons names, and each one was up to 20 characters long, we could declare e.g:

```
char name [200] [20];
```

In fact, this can be regarded as an array of 200 elements, each one of which is an array of 20 characters. In C, we can refer to the complete name of a person by, e.g:

```
name[150]
```

i.e it is not illegal to use only one subscript. This is useful in certain cases, but you need to read chapter 13 to use the technique properly. Briefly, every name will not be exactly 20 characters long, so a terminator character is stored, leaving up to 19 characters for the name.

12.4 Functions and Pointers

So far, we have have seen that functions

- can have arguments – whose values are copied into the function.
- can return a result.

What if a function must return several results ? Recalling our use of scanf and printf may emphasize this concept. If we put:

```
printf("%d %d %d", count,sum,salary);
```

all that printf needs ia a copy of the values in the 3 variables.

But if we put:

```
scanf("%d%d%d",&age,&weight,&height);
```

what happens is that the user will type in values at the keyboard – what does scanf do with them? It needs to know where to put them, i.e. it needs the addresses of the 3 variables.

Here is an analogy – a manager passes 3 amounts of money (the 3 values) to an assistant, and asks for them to be delivered to the correct rooms. The assistant needs to ask – where?
Obviously it is not possible to work out where the money should go from looking at the amounts of money.

Similarly, in scanf we use the address operator & before variable names. This causes the address of the variable to be passed to the function, rather than the value. If a function has the address, it can put a new value at that address.

Note that when we code up a function to which addresses (rather than values) are to be passed, the body of the function will often need to use the pointer operator * .

Here is an example: we will code a function which accepts two integer values, and returns their sum and difference.

There are two important features in this problem:

- we only need to pass the values of the two integers into the function; these values are not to be changed.
- there are two results, which means we need to use &. If we only required one result, we could have dispensed with & and used 'return'.

Here is a complete program, showing the function and how it might be called.

```
/* returning several results - example    */
#include <stdio.h>

void sum_diff();

main()
{
    int c,d,x,y,add,subtract;
    c = 9;              /* assign demonstration values */
    d = 12;
    sum_diff(3,21,&x,&y);              /* call 1 */
    sum_diff(c,d,&add,&subtract);      /* call 2 */
}
```

```
/*****************************************/
/* given a,b - calculates a+b , a-b     */
void sum_diff(a,b,sum,diff)
int a,b;
int *sum,*diff;
{
   *sum = a+b;
   *diff = a-b;
}
/*****************************************/
```

Here is what takes place:
a and b are passed by value , as usual.

The other two arguments need to be addresses – this way of passing is often termed 'passing by reference'.

```
int *sum,*diff;
```

declares two variables that will hold addresses of items – i.e. they are pointers.

When we want to affect the item that is pointed at, we use *, as in:

```
*diff = a+b;
```

* means 'de–reference' the pointer, and in other contexts it also means multiply.

At this stage it is reasonable to ask what

```
diff = a+b;
```

would do. Recall that when variables are declared, an address in RAM will be used (see Appendix 1). For example, x may exist in location 3320, and y may exist in 3321. The actual numbers are not important, and they are allocated by the C compiler. Our first call is:

```
sum_diff(3,21,&x,&y);
```

The values are transferred, i.e:

a becomes 3, b becomes 21, sum becomes 3320, diff becomes 3321.

Focussing on diff, we say that it points to y. If we put

```
diff = a-b;
```

diff becomes 3 - 21 i.e -18. What does diff point to now ? It is unlikely that anything useful exists at a negative location, and on many machines an addressing error may arise.

What we wanted to do was to place -18 in y, i.e. the place that diff points to. This is done by:

```
*diff = a-b;
```

Here are some incorrect calls:

```
sum_diff(3,21,&x,y);
sum_diff(3,21,&x,4);
```

In both cases, we are not passing a sensible address for the fourth argument. Unfortunately, C may not detect this mis-use, and debugging will be needed.

Finally, note the style of the call. We can't use sum_diff as part of an expression :

```
n = sum_diff(3,21,&x,&y) +88;
```

The way we have coded sum_diff determines that the call must make up a complete statement.

The Big Picture

- A C style has evolved for certain types of functions, involving the use of arguments to pass values into a function, the use of & to pass results back, and the use of return to pass back a status code. The nature of this returned value depends on the particular function, but typically it is a small integer, whose value may signify e.g:
  - function worked OK
  - function couldn't handle the input values
  - something went wrong- e.g a file was missing from disk.

  etc

As an example, you could find from a reference manual that scanf, as well as storing values typed at the keyboard, returns the number of correct data items stored. Thus we may put:

```
if ( scanf("%d%d", &x,&y) != 2 )
    /* take some error action */
else
    /* worked OK */
```

The use of scanf to detect input errors is described in the 'C Miscellany' chapter.

- Recall that when an array is passed as a function argument, the address of the first element is passed. Thus, we have a value which tells us where something exists in memory. Yes – a pointer! To obtain the element number 2 in an array, we put:

```
x = a[2];
```

but the same task could be expressed with pointers. For example, if the pointer pa also pointed at the first element of the array, adding 2 to it will reference element 2. (Remember that we count from zero in C).

```
x = *(p+2);
```

- C allows functions to be written which accept a variable number of arguments. (printf() is such a function.) The technique is not described here.

Key Points

- In most circumstances, 2-dimensional array elements are selected by 2 subscripts: [ ] [ ]

- Functions can accept 2-dimensional arrays as arguments. For highly-specific functions, the array row and column sizes can be specified in the function. For general-purpose functions, we need to fix the length of a row.

- If a function needs to return several values, consider using pointers. Alternatively, the function could doing too much! Consider splitting it up into smaller functions.

Problems

1. Write a program which sets the array int a[10] [10] to the pattern:

```
1 0 0 0 ...etc
0 1 0 0
0 0 1 0
.
etc
```

   Print out the array to check the result.

2. Using the array float data [10] [10] write a simplified spreadsheet program (without formula facilities). It should accept the following commands:

   p print the whole array

   r 3 requests the user to enter a column of numbers, and stores them in the specified column (e.g. 3).

   + 2 3 adds columns element by element, leaving the result in the first-mentioned column. Here, row 3 is added to row 2.

   * 2 5.3 multiplies each element in a column by the specified float value. Here column 2 is multiplied by 5.3

   s stop

3. Write a program which produces a histogram of 12 monthly rainfall figures, in the form

```
                  ... etc
6       ***          ***
5       ***          ***
4       *** ***      ***
3       *** ***      ***
2       *** *** *** ***
1       *** *** *** ***
        Jan Feb Mar Apr      etc
```

   Assume that no rainfall value exceeds 20, and use a char array of 20 by 48 to build up the picture.

4. As Q3, but allow any range of values. Scale the data suitably by firstly finding the largest value. Note that very small figures should also be scaled up.

CHAPTER 13
CHARACTER STRINGS

Introduction

String manipulation is a very frequent task in programming – e.g. the manipulation of names and addresses, the compilation of a program into machine language etc. Facilities are not built in, but the language was designed so that string functions could be written in C and then incorporated into any program. Thus there is a standard library of functions available on most C systems.

In C, strings are basically arrays of characters, so we could create space for a string by, e.g:

```
char animal[4];
```

and could give it a value by:

```
animal[0] = 'c';
animal[1] = 'a';
animal[2] = 't';
animal[3] = '\0';
```

Note that all C's string-handling functions expect strings to be terminated by a character-code of zero (i.e 00000000, often called NULL) and we represent this in C by the escape code \0

If we wanted to print the string on the screen, we can use the 's' format in printf, as in:

```
printf("%s", animal);
```

where cat would be printed.
Let us now look at the detail.

13.1 Declaring String Variables

We estimate the maximum number of characters that the string will need to hold, and also allow space for the terminator. If we were dealing with a person's name, we might put

```
char person_name[50];
```

We may also use 'static' with arrays, which (among other things) allows us to declare and initialise simultaneously, as in:

```
char address[] = "3 Smith Road, Sheffield";
```

Note the use of double quotes. They cause a null terminator to be put at the end. If we don't supply a size in [ ], C will calculate it for us. Note that the item 'x' in single quotes is not a character string in C, it is a single character, whereas "x" in double quotes is a character string consisting of one character followed by the terminator.

13.2 String I/O

We can use printf and scanf with the "%s" format. Thus, to read a name from the keyboard, we could put:

```
scanf("%s" , person_name);
```

Note that we don't use & before the string (array) name when passing it to scanf. Behind the scenes, C passes the address of the first character, so we don't need the explicit '&' address operator.

Scanf treats spaces and newlines ('white space') as string separators, so if the user typed the name:

Bruce Springsteen

then person_name would be set to "Bruce". If we wanted to read the full name, we could put:

```
char first_name[50], last_name[50];
    ...
scanf("%s%s" , first_name , last_name);
```

Output is straightforward – e.g. to print the name, followed by a newline, use :

```
printf("%s\n" , person_name);
```

13.3 The String Library

On many C systems, this is available to the programmer without explicitly putting

```
#include <string.h>
```

at the start – check your particular system manual for details. Here, we will assume that it is needed.

In your system documentation on string functions, you might see variable declarations such as:

```
char *fred;
```

The * means 'pointer to', i.e that fred contains the address of the start of a character string. The * indicates a pointer; suffice it to say that:

```
char *fred;
```

is very similar to

```
char fred[n];
```

In each case, using 'fred' as a function argument results in the start address in RAM being passed to the function, enabling the function to locate the successive elements by repeatedly adding 1 to the start address.

We will look at some of the string functions, together with examples of their use. Assume the declarations:

```
char first_name[] = "Bruce";
char last_name[] = "Springsteen";
char person_name[50];
char command[10];
int n;
```

■ String length - strlen

e.g:

```
printf("length is %d",strlen( first_name) );
```

where 'Length is 5' is printed.

```
if ( strlen(last_name) > 12 )
    etc
```

■ String copy - strcpy

This gives the effect of string assignment. In C, we can't copy whole strings by putting:

```
person_name=last_name;/* doesn't do what you think ! */
```

Instead, we put:

```
strcpy(person_name , last_name);
```

We can also use a quoted string:

```
strcpy(person_name, "Kate Bush");
```

■ String joining (concatenation) - strcat

To join s2 to the end of s1, we put

```
strcat(s1,s2);
```

e.g:
```
strcpy(person_name,"Jack ");
strcat(person_name, first_name);
```

and we find that first_name is now – "Jack Bruce".

■ String comparison – strcmp

Here, the returned integer value is important. When we compare two strings s1 , s2 , the result is:

0 if they are identical.

negative if s1 is 'before' s2 in dictionary (lexicographic) order.

positive(>0) if s2 is before s1.

Thus if we had:

```
if (  strcmp(first_name,last_name) <0  )
    ...
```

The result would be negative, as "B" is before "S" in lexicographic order. This function is common when testing for a command from the user, eg:
```
scanf("%s" , command );
if ( strcmp(command, "quit")==0  )
    ...
else if ( strcmp(command,"go")==0 )
    ...
```

The Big Picture

■ Arrays of strings. In C we can declare arrays in which each element is itself a character string, as in:

```
char  name_list[100] [20];
```

Here, we set up an array of 100 elements, each of which can hold a string of up to 19 characters and its terminator. We may now use statements of the form:

```
scanf("%s", name_list[0]);      /* nb no & */
strcpy(name_list[1], "Springsteen" );
strcpy(name_list[2], name_list[0]);
strcpy(name_list[3], name_list[1]);
if ( strcmp(name_list[2], name_list[3]) )
        etc
```

which reads a string into element 0, copies a string into element 1, copies element 0 into element 2, element 1 into element 3, then compares elements 2 and 3. Note that we should not write statements of the form:

```
name_list[2] = name_list[0];
if ( name_list[2] == name_list[3] )
```

Key Points

- Strings are arrays of char, with the end marked by a special terminator character.
- The length of a string can vary throughout the run of a program, but we must choose its maximum length.
- Use functions to manipulate strings – check your particular library for additional useful functions.

Problems

1. Write a program to compare two strings typed in at the keyboard. Print either 'identical' or 'different'.
2. Write a program which reads a series of words separated by white space, and which prints the length of the longest one. Assume that the last word is "STOP".

3. Write a program to implement a primitive spelling checker. The input is as in Q2. When a word is encountered, the program should either:

   - print it if it hasn't been used before, or
   - produce no output if it has been used before.

   Thus, the output is a list of words which occur at least once in the input. The writer will then examine the list for errors. Use an array of strings.

CHAPTER 14
MODULES
AND OBJECTS

Introduction

Software systems are very large and complex – some can be 1 million lines of code, with lots of interactions between different areas. It is essential to break up such software into separate parts. Here we will look at the technique of separate compilation, then at the increasingly popular approach of modules.

14.1 Scopes

The scope of an item (e.g. a variable) is the range of the program in which it may be used. Thus, in:

```
/*  e.g. of scopes */
int g;
void f1();
main()
{
    int lm;
}

void f1()
{
    int lf1;
    int g;
    g = 123;      /*  which g  ?  */
}
```

we see the familar local(automatic) scope of lm (local to main only) and lf1(local to f1 only). Less familar is the scope of g declared near the top of the file. In fact it is global and can be used by any function in the file (here we have main and f1). The C jargon is external, i.e. outside every function. Look at the use of g in f1. Will the global or local variable be used? In C, the local one is selected. Whilst on the subject of large systems, it is likely that programmers will work independently on different functions – it is worth recalling that they are free to invent local names without checking that they have been named elsewhere. If two programmers choose the same name in two functions, then two separate variables will be used – i.e. no problem of interaction. There is one other important scope, known as 'external static' which will be introduced by example.

14.2 Separate Compilation

As you are aware, C has a large collection of previously-compiled functions in libraries, which can be incorporated in your programs. However, if the source text of your program becomes large and cumbersome (and maybe slow to compile) you might adopt the same approach of separating out a function, and compiling it independently. Assuming that the function is correct, it will only need recompiling occasionally.

Here is an example: we have a main program in a file called main.c, which calls accounts() and payroll(). Assume they have no arguments, for simplicity.

```
/* file:  main.c */
int accounts();  /* declarations */
void payroll();

main()
{
...
}

int accounts()
{
...
}
```

```
void payroll()
{
   /* lots of  C  code */
...
}
```

Assume that payroll() is very large, and seems to be correct – we decide to use separate compilation. What we do is to use a text editor to put it in its own file, say payroll.c, and we also delete it from main.c. The exact details of the following system commands vary, but the principles are similar. We now compile (but don't run) payroll.c, producing a compiled file called payroll.o ('o' for 'object code'). The main.c file is now reduced to:

```
/* file:  main.c */
int accounts();             /* declarations */
extern void payroll();  /* NB extern     */
main()
{
...
}

int accounts()
{
...
}
```

Note the use of 'extern' in the declaration of payroll, meaning that the definition of it will be found in another file.

We may now compile and run main.c. additionally telling the system to link in the previously–compiled payroll.o file.

On some systems:
    cc main.c payroll.o

14.3 Modules and Objects

The terms 'module' and 'object' have come to mean a collection of functions, along with the data they manipulate. The concept is fundamental to the languages Smalltalk and C++ (yes – one up from C!) though the arguments about why is is beneficial are not developed here.

As an example of a software object, consider the cursor on a screen. We manipulate it by pressing keys or moving a mouse, but behind the scenes, the system software has to maintain its coordinates. Thus, the object has code associated with it, and an internal state, i.e the values of its concealed x/y position.

C is not ideal for this style of programming, but it does allow us to separate out a collection of functions together with the variables they use.

Here is an example: we require to keep track of the balance in a bank account, which is manipulated by the functions pay_in, withdraw, and fetch_balance. We will need a variable to keep track of the current balance – call it 'balance'. We have

```
/* file: all_bank_account.c */
void pay_in();         /* declarations */
void withdraw();
float fetch_balance();

main()
{
   ...
}

void pay_in(amount)
float amount;
{
   balance = balance + amount;
}

void withdraw(amount)
float amount;
{
   ...
}

float fetch_balance()
{
   ...
}
...
lots of other functions  which don't use balance
...
```

The problem is where do we declare: float balance; ?

We can't declare it in every function as a local – we only want one copy of it. We could declare it above the main program, so that it was global to all the functions in the file. However, we know that only 3 functions use it – why make it available to the whole program?

The solution is a 'module', which is created as follows: use a text editor to separate out the text of the 3 functions, and put them in a new file (e.g. balance_module.c). We have:

```
/* file:  balance_module.c */
static float balance=0.0;  /*  declare and init. */

void pay_in(amount);
float amount;
{
   balance = balance + amount;
}

and the code for withdraw, fetch_balance:-
... etc.
```

The variable 'balance' now exists for all time (it is not a local) but can only be used by the 3 functions in balance_module.c, not by any others in the file all_bank_account.c. The module can now be compiled. Finally, we would modify the three declarations in all_bank_account.c to:

```
/*  file:  all_bank_account.c  */
extern void pay_in();      /*  declarations */
extern void withdraw();
extern float fetch_balance();
```

then compile it and link to the module as shown earlier. Note that balance is not declared in all_bank_account.c.

Thus we have a module made up of a variable, and its associated functions, rather than having them scattered throughout a large file. If we now wanted to alter part of the software which dealt with balance (perhaps so that it was stored on disc), we would only alter the module file, not the main file. This makes maintenance easier.

14.4 Headers

In the above, we needed to get the three function declarations correct, to ensure that any results from the functions were handled properly. To make it easier for others to use your functions, you could put the 3 lines in a header file called e.g. balance_module.h:

```
/* file: balance_module.h */
extern void pay_in();       /*  declarations */
extern void withdraw();
extern float fetch_balance();
```

and simply tell other users to include this at the top of their program, as in:

```
/*  file:  all_bank_account.c  */
#include "balance_module.h"
```

Key Points

- Header files (.h) files typically contain declarations for functions which will be linked in at a later stage.
- Consider using separate compilation for sets of related functions which manipulate common variables or I/O devices,

Problems

1. Write a set of functions which manipulate a simple English – French dictionary, containing two arrays of strings e.g:

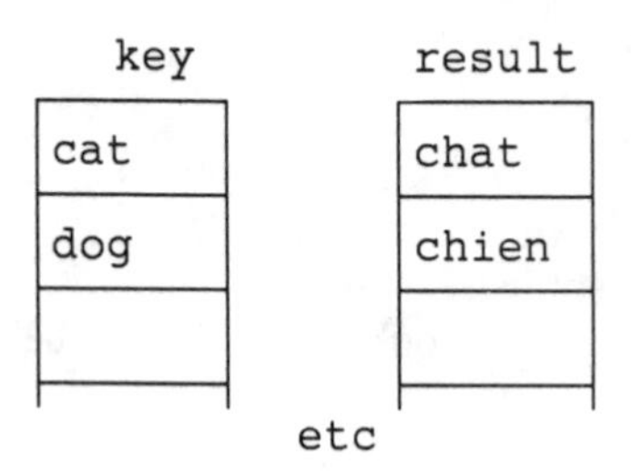

Your functions should perform such tasks as:

- initialise the dictionary
- find if an English word exists in key[]
- return the French equivalent
- insert a new pair of words
- delete a pair of words

    etc

Make use of separate compilation.

CHAPTER 15
C MISCELLANY

Introduction

In this chapter, we will take a brief look at some additional C facilities which do not warrant full coverage in an introductory text. C is a 'real-life' language, which can cope with the messy detail needed in some software systems; for example - bit manipulation, efficient coding, access to filing systems, and the detection of input errors. In addition, we will look at popular idioms. Just as one can't be perfect in a human language by merely learning grammar, so there are styles of using C use which would not be apparent from a reference manual.

15.1 Bit Manipulation

C can perform tasks that would traditionally be done in assembler language. There are additional 'bitwise' operators, which allow the programmer to access the bits within a word. Here we will look briefy at what is possible, but note that a knowledge of binary arithmetic is assumed. If you really want to use C in a practical application at this low level, it is likely that you have this already.

The operators are:

```
~       ones complement
&       bitwise and
|       bitwise or
^       bitwise exclusive or
>>      bitwise shift right
<<      bitwise shift left
```

The and, or, exclusive or operators implement the familiar boolean logic concepts, but they do it on the corresponding bits of two words. So if we 'or' the two patterns:

11000000 00000111

we get

11000111

Here are some examples on 8-bit bytes, which also illustrate the coding of hexadecimal numbers by prefixing them with 0x.

```
/* assume a is initially 00001111               */
b = ~a;           /* b is 11110000              */
c = a & 0x3;      /* a and 11 is  00000011      */
d = a | 0xF0;     /* a and 11110000 is 11111111 */
e = a >>2;        /* e is 00000011              */
f = a << 3;       /* f is 01111000              */
```

Here is an example: a printer sets a status byte in the following manner:

bit 0 - (the rightmost bit) - 1 if the paper is low.
bit 2 - 1 if the paper is jammed.
bits 1, 3, 4, 5, 6, 7 are unused, but but could be set to <u>any</u> value - we need to ignore them explicitly.

Assume that the status has been loaded into s. We can mask out the unwanted bits by 'anding' with 00000101:

```
useful = s & 0x05;
```

We could access the 'jammed' bit by anding, or by shifting the 'low' bit off to the right:

```
jammed_bit = useful >> 2;
```

or

```
jammed_bit = useful & 0x04;  /* 00000100  */
```

It is important not to confuse the bitwise & | with the logical && ||. Unless you are specifically accessing the bits in a word, use && ||.

15.2 Efficiency

When we code such statements as:

```
n = n+1;
```

the compiler is likely to generate machine code of the form:

```
fetch n
add 1
store result back in n
```

but many computers are in fact able to do the above task in one hardware instruction, e.g:

```
increment n
```

Such an instruction can only be used when the same variable occurs on either side of =.

C allows us to put:

```
n++;        /* add 1 to  n */
```

which is likely to be faster and take up less space in the machine code version. We also have the corresponding -- operator for decrementing by 1. So far, so good – we have a concise and efficient notation. The problem (from the learning aspect) is that we can use the operators in a pre-increment or post-increment way, as in:

```
i++;
j--;
--k;
--l;
```

There is a straightforward use of these operators: when we use them as a complete statement. Thus, to add 1 to n we may put:

```
n = n+1;      n++;        ++n;
```

However, be wary when the resulting value is used. Consider:

```
int m,n;
m = 0;
n = 0;
printf("%d%d\n", m++ , ++n );
```

The printed result is: 0 1
because in the post-increment (m++) form, the original value is used for printf, then the ++ adds 1. With the pre-increment form (++n) the addition takes place before the resulting value is passed to printf.

Similarly, we have:

```
n = 0;
m = 0;
a = m++;        /* a becomes 0, m becomes 1 */
b = ++n;        /* b becomes 1, n becomes 1 */
```

Another frequent pattern which has a fast machine code equivalent is that of:

```
n = n +   some expression;
```

There are several assignment operators in addition to =, the most popular being:

```
+=     -=
```

For example, we could write:

```
i += 5*w*t;   /* means  i = i +(5*w*t);  */
n -= 3+s;     /* means  n = n -(3+s);    */
```

The choice is yours! You can use either the concise compact notation – which may be harder to follow in certain cases, or the more long-winded form. There is little hard evidence to help you – experienced C programmers become used to using and reading the compact form, but those who are familiar with say Cobol or Pascal will find them objectionable.

15.3 Conditions and Assignment

We know what the + operator does in:

```
4 + 3
```

it operates on 4 and 3, producing the result 7

Consider

```
x = 3;
```

One thing that = does is to store 3 in x, but a secondary effect takes place. The statement has a result – the value that is assigned. We can use this result in expressions.

For example:

```
printf("%d" , x = 3);
```

Here, x is given the value 3, which is also the result of the expression, hence '3' is printed. We could get the same effect by:

```
x = 3;
printf"%d" , x);
```

i.e. 2 statements instead of one. This latter form will be less confusing for people who don't work exclusively in C.

15.4 Using = in Conditions.

Consider:

```
x = 99;
if (x=3)
    ...
```

This is correct C syntax – but what does it mean ? Firstly, for the purpose of the example, we put 99 in x. Then, in the bracketed condition, we assign 3 to x, and test the result of the assignment (which is 3) for true or false. 3 is non-zero, i.e. true, so the condition is evaluated as true. Whether the programmer meant this to happen is doubtful - perhaps the code should have been:

```
x = 99;
if (x==3)
    ...
```

which evaluates to false. It is very easy to mis-type = instead of ==, and C accepts it, treating it as an assignment. The drawback in C is that == and = look similar, but do totally different things.

Here is an example of a common C idiom. The problem is to copy some input text from the keyboard to the screen, assuming that the text ends with a ';'.

In most languages, we would come up with logic along the lines of:

```
c = getchar();
while ( c != ';' )
{
    putchar(c);
    c = getchar();
}
```

Many C programmers would combine the read and the test:

```
while ( (c = getchar() ) != ';' )
{
    putchar(c)
}
```

The extra brackets round c=getchar() are needed to force it to be evaluated first, rather than evaluating getchar()!=';'. The braces enclose a single statement and could be omitted.

15.5 End Of File.

Whilst on the topic of the getchar/putchar loop, note that the above problem was simplified. More typically, we will be dealing with a stream of characters, perhaps piped from another program. The convention is that a special character will mark the end of the stream. However, this conflicts with the requirement of a flexible filing system, which needs to be able to store any characters within a file. For example, if the convention was that $ marked the end, we wouldn't be able to use $ within the file .

Recall that characters occupy one byte, and have integer codes from 0 to 255. On most C systems, end of file is marked by the value −1, which (on a 16 bit system) is represented by the binary pattern:

1111111111111111

On most C systems, the end of file 'magic number' is #defined as EOF. The code to read a stream of characters is now:

```
int c;
while ((c = getchar() ) != EOF)
    putchar(c);
```

Note that c is int, not char, because it needs to hold a 16 bit number – albeit only once!

An additional example of the assignment/condition idiom can be seen in the following section.

15.6 File Input – Output

Many programs need to refer to named data files, In the Unix OS, we can write programs which accept I/O from a variety of sources, but we may still need to refer to actual named files from time to time.

Here is a program which reads a series of integers from the file "fred.data" and which prints them on the screen. The data file would be created with a text editor.

```
/*  eg of file reading  */
#include <stdio.h>
main()
{
    int number;
    FILE  *fpointer;     /* FILE is in stdio */
```

```
    /* open for reading  "r" */
    fpointer = fopen("fred.data" , "r");

    /* while not end of file */
    while ( ! feof(fpointer) )
    {

        /* read number from file */
        fscanf(fpointer , "%d" , &number);

        printf("%d\n", number);
    }

    fclose(fpointer);
}
```

We set up a 'file pointer' variable for each file, and use the fopen function to associate a file name with the pointer. There are several file-handling functions, but here we have restricted ourselves to testing for end of file, using fscanf (the file version of scanf) and closing the file when we have finished.

One possibility is that a file doesn't exist when we try to read from it. It is good practice to trap such error cases, and fopen allows this, by returning a NULL result in an error case. (NULL is zero on most systems, and is #defined in stdio.h) We could put:

```
fpointer = fopen("fred.data" , "r");
if (fpointer == NULL)
    printf("error in opening file\n");
...etc
```

or, as is very common, use the C idiom of assignment in conditions:

```
if ( (fpointer = fopen("fred.data" , "r") ) == NULL)
    printf("error in opening file");
... etc
```

Your C manual will provide details of the full range of file I/O functions.

15.7 Input Errors

As you know, there are two styles of calling functions – as part of an expression, or as a complete statement. For example, using the library functions sqrt and scanf, we usually put e.g:

```
x=sqrt(16.0);
scanf("%d", &n);
```

We would no more think of putting:

```
sqrt(16.0);
```

as a statement by itself than of putting:

```
4.0;
```

However, some of the library functions, particularly those involving I/O, can be used in two ways. Your manuals will give details, but here we look at scanf. Let us declare some variables and read some data from the user:

```
int n,a;
float x;
char ch;

scanf("%d%f%c" , &a, &x, &ch);
```

Here, scanf reads an int, a float, and a char. assigning the values to a, x and ch.
Thus, if the user typed:

```
65 83.2
```

on a single line, 65 is assigned to a, 83.2 is assigned to x, and the end-of-line character is assigned to ch.
If the data is:

```
65 83.2w
```

then similar results occur, except ch now holds 'w'. Note that the input data is still correct – a number is ended by a non-digit.

But we can put:

```
n=scanf("%d%f%c" , &a,&x,&ch);
```

The result of scanf (which we have stored in n) is the number of successful assignments made using the input data. In the above, with no input errors, n becomes 3.
This facility enables the programmer to check for input errors – here is some input data for the above scanf call, and the resulting value of n:

```
12 34.5,              n is 3
12 ,x                 n is 1
abc                   n is 0
```

What happens is that as soon as scanf hits an error in the input data, it stops immediately, without reading any more characters. This is sensible, but it means that the programmer must be careful in handling the error: it is not sufficient to simply repeat the scanf call, because reading will commence from the incorrect character found previously, and a second error is likely.

Here is an example: we wish to input two floats, followed by an end-of-line character.

```
float f1,f2;
int n;
char last,ignore;            /*see below for usage */

n = scanf("%f%f%c" , &f1, &f2, &last);
```

If n turns out to be 3, and last holds the end-of-line (\n) character, there is no problem. Incidentally, scanf will also accept the two numbers on separate lines. But if the user types:

```
abc  123.4
```

then n will become 0, because scanf stops whilst attempting to find a float to store in f1. The error data is not skipped over, so scanf is still positioned before the 'a'. Repeating the same scanf will cause an identical error because of the 'a'.

There are a variety of ways to 'tidy up' after such an error. One is to ignore all the following data on the input line, and invite the user to type the whole line again. To ignore the data, we can read it as characters with scanf – if we try to read it as numbers, errors will obviously occur.

Assuming there has been a scanf error, here is how to read the rest of the line, up to and including the end-of-line character.

```
while(ignore != '\n' )
{
    scanf("%c" , &ignore);
}
```

We can now prompt the user to retype the data, and read it with the same scanf call.

15.8 Structures

Frequently, a single variable is not suitable to hold a data item. For example, we might wish to manipulate data concerned with peoples' ages and names, i.e. two items, each of a different type. It would be possible to use two variables, but in C we may use a structure:

```
struct person_data
    {
        int age;
        char name[20];
    };
```

Here we have declared a structure – the pattern for a new kind of variable, with two 'members', called age and name. As yet no variables have been declared, merely a pattern. Later in the program we can actually declare the variables:

```
struct person_data  employee, manager,worker[10];
```

Now we have employee, manager and an array of 10 workers, each with name and age. We can now access the individual parts (i.e. members) by:

```
manager.age = 59;
employee.name = "Hendrix";
worker[6].age = 18;      /* age of worker 6  */
```

In addition, we can assign complete structures:

```
employee = worker[6];
```

It might help you to understand the use of '.' to imagine it as 's, giving:

manager's age = 59;

In more advanced programs, you will encounter structure variables that have no name – all we know is where they are in RAM, i.e. a pointer. Thus, if p points to a structure in the form of person_data, we may put:

```
n = p -> age;  /* extract the age from the structure */
```

The -> is typed as two characters.

Problems

1. Write a function called read_correct_float which has no arguments and returns a float result. It should read a float number from the keyboard. As long as an incorrect float is entered, a message requesting the user to re-type the number should be displayed. For the purposes of this problem, a correct float is one which scanf() accepts, and which is followed immediately by an end-of-line character.

2. Write a program which prints a table of 8-bit decimal integers with their binary equivalents, e.g:

```
0          00000000
1          00000001
   etc
255        11111111
```

3. Write a program to produce an overview of the 'outer' logic of a C program stored in a file. A primitive way to do this is to replace a series of lines that are indented by more than n spaces by:

   ...

   Allow the user to supply a value for n, and write the output to a second file.

CHAPTER 16
CASE STUDY

Introduction

Here we look at the development of a complete program, from initial conception through to pseudocode design and C coding. It doesn't use every feature that we have covered, but does manage to incorporate functions, arguments, results, and arrays. The program is an interactive game called 'Reverse' - not the most exciting game you have ever played, but more interesting than games in which the computer simply simulates the toss of a coin or throw of a dice. Note that the following pseudocode uses the C assignment (=) and 'for' statement. They were avoided in our initial look at pseudocode, but can sensibly be incorporated at this stage. However, we will still omit low-level detail.

16.1 The Game of Reverse

Basically, the computer will display a row of 5 numbers, and the player types in commands in an attempt to re-arrange (i.e. sort) the numbers into ascending order in a small number of moves. Here is an example:

```
 1   2   3   4   5
32  18  16  52  81
```

The player can re-arrange the numbers by a 'reverse' command, in which a sequence of numbers starting from the left is reversed. In the above, we could choose to reverse:

1 through to 2, or
1 through to 3, or
1 through to 4, or
1 through to 5

The best choice is 1 to 3, giving:

1	2	3	4	5
16	18	32	52	81

However, if we started with

1	2	3	4	5
32	61	50	79	83

then the problem is not so simple – we aren't allowed to reverse 2 and 3 directly, so several steps are needed – e.g. reverse 3, then 2, then 3.

The basic idea of the game is therefore that the program keeps track of the current state of the numbers – it doesn't play tactically. To implement it on a computer we need to be more specific:

- the program will count the number of reversing attempts made by the player.
- we will use 5 numbers, and number them 1 to 5 (not 0 to 4). Most humans count from 1 upwards. However we may want to increase the numbers above 5 in a future version, so #define will be useful.
- instructions will be printed out on request.
- the program will stop when the sorting is complete, and will print the number of reversing attempts.
- a 'quit' command will allow the user to stop at any time.
- incorrect commands will be rejected.

At this stage, we could think about menus, graphics etc (from a C library), for command input, but to simplify the coding and to make the program machine-independent, single-letter commands will be adopted, i.e:

q	–	quit
i	–	print instructions
r	–	reverse – a prompt for the number to be reversed will follow, and the user will enter in number in the range 1 to 5.

16.2 The Design

After some time spent struggling with pencil and paper, the following main program was arrived at:

```
initialise_row
display_row
attempt_count = 0
get_valid_command
while command not 'q'   and   row not sorted
    obey_command
    get_valid_command
endwhile
if sorted
    print attempt_count with congratulations
endif
```

After close examination, a bug was found in the above – we really need to check for a sorted row immediately after obey_command. In the above, the order of execution is:

```
obey_command
get_valid_command
check if sorted (in the while condition)
```

This is a case where 'while' is not suitable – the steps should be:

```
get_valid_command
obey_command
check if sorted
```

The easiest way to provide this is to use a do–while, in which the test for continuing comes at the bottom of the loop, as in:

```
do
    ...
while (condition)
```

Fortunately, this logic error was spotted at an early stage, so very little of the design (and none of the C code) needs re-working. The improved version is:

```
initialise_row
display_row
attempt_count = 0
do
    get_valid_command
    obey_command
while command not 'q'   and     row not sorted
if sorted
    print attempt_count with congratulations
endif
```

Moving on to lower levels, 'initialise_row' involves putting suitable values in the row. An array is the obvious structure, with element zero unused. If several players were competing, they would all require the same numbers, so we will fix these by assignment statements. Alternatively, we could use a random number generator ('rand()' function) but would need to reject duplicate numbers, and any sequences that were sorted already.

The function 'display_row' is again trivial – we have enough experience to know that printing out an array is no major task.

The function get_valid_command consists of reading a command. Later, you will be asked to incorporate validity checking.

The function 'obey_command' chooses which function to call:

```
obey_command consists of:
    if command is 'q'
        quit
    else
        if command is 'i'
            print_instructions
        else
            if command is 'i'
                do_reverse
            endif
        endif
    endif
end of function
```

We now need to plan the reversing and checking tasks. Firstly, if we reverse an even number of values, e.g. 4:

55 66 44 33

there will be 2 interchanges (55 with 33, 66 with 44). But what if the player chooses an odd number e.g 5 ? Here is an example:

55 66 22 44 33

We still do 2 interchanges, because there is no need to interchange 22 with itself. Thus, with an odd number, we divide by 2 and round down to calculate the number of interchanges. The C operator / does this very thing.

```
function do_reverse consists of:
    get reverse_count from user
    interchanges = reverse_count / 2
    for(n=1 ; n <= interchanges; n = n+1 )
        interchange row[n] with row[reverse_count]
        reverse_count= reverse_count - 1
    endfor
    attempt_count = attempt_count+1
    display_row
end of function
```

The remaining significant task is the checking of row, to detect a finished game. The numbers are sorted if element 2 is bigger than element 1, element 3 is bigger than element 2, etc. Conversly, they are unsorted if we find a pair where the rightmost value is smaller. The possibility of duplicates ought not to occur! We have:

```
row_sorted consists of:
    sorted = true              /* assumed, to get loop going */
    n = 1
    while n<5   and   sorted
        if row[n+1]<=row[n]
            sorted = false
        else
            n = n+1
        endif
    endwhile
    return sorted              /* i.e.  true or false  */
end of function
```

We have now sketched out the main logic, but several issues remain, e.g:

- scope of variables (local, global etc)
- arguments, results from functions.
- use of #define to make the program easy to modify.
- separate compilation (more applicable in larger programs)
- validation (checking) of input commands. Good checking can involve substantial programming!
- C style. An experienced C programmer would combine some of the while/if/assignment statements.

The C coding is shown overleaf.

16.3 Reverse in C

```
/* The Game Of Reverse */
/*Mike Parr - June 90  */

#include <stdio.h>

/* Booleans*/

#define BOOLEAN int
#define TRUE 1
#define FALSE 0

/* Allow row array to be accessed from 1 to ROW_SIZE */
#define ROW_SIZE 6

/* Function Declarations */

void initialise_row();
BOOLEAN row_sorted();
char get_valid_command();
void obey_command();
void quit();
void display_row();
void do_reverse();
void interchange();
void initialise_row();
void print_instructions();


/* Globals */

int row[ROW_SIZE];
int attempt_count;
```

```
main()
{
   char command;

   printf("Welcome to the game of reverse.\n");
   printf("Type  i  for instructions.\n");

   initialise_row();
   display_row();
   attempt_count = 0;

   do
   {
      command = get_valid_command();
      obey_command(command);
   }
   while ( (command != 'q') && !row_sorted() );

   if (row_sorted() )
   {
      printf("Congratulations!\n");
      printf("Done in  %d goes.\n" , attempt_count);
   }
}


/************************************************/
/*  display_row: displays row and positions     */
/************************************************/

void display_row()
{
   int n;
   /* print positions  */
   for(n = 1; n < ROW_SIZE; n++)
      printf("%4d",n);
   printf("\n");

   /* print actual numbers */
   for(n = 1; n < ROW_SIZE; n++)
      printf("%4d" , row[n]);
   printf("\n");
}
```

```
/************************************************/
/* get_valid_command - returns the command char   */
/************************************************/

char get_valid_command()
{           /* a reduced 'stub' of the final version*/
   char c, ignore;
   printf("Type command: ");
   scanf("%c%c", &c, &ignore);
   return c;
}

/************************************************/
/* obey_command - depending on its char argument  */
/************************************************/
void obey_command(command)
char command;
{
   if (command=='q')
      quit();
   else if (command=='i')
      print_instructions();
   else if (command=='r')
      do_reverse();
}

/************************************************/
/* do_reverse - reverses the specified number     */
/************************************************/
void do_reverse()
{
   int interchanges;
   int n;
   int reverse_count;

   reverse_count = get_reverse();
   interchanges = reverse_count / 2;
   for(n = 1; n <= interchanges; n++)
   {
      interchange(&row[n] , &row[reverse_count]);
      reverse_count--;
   }
   attempt_count++;
   display_row();
}
```

```
/***********************************************/
/*  get_reverse- returns a valid reversing number */
/***********************************************/

int get_reverse()
{
   int reverse;
   char ignore;
   printf("How many to reverse? ");
   while ( (scanf("%d%c", &reverse, &ignore) !=2)
         || (reverse<0 || reverse > ROW_SIZE-1) )
   {
      while (ignore !='\n')
         scanf("%c", &ignore);
      printf("Error in number - re-enter it please: ");
   }

   return reverse;
}


/***********************************************/
/* interchange - swaps elements during reversing  */
/***********************************************/

void interchange(x,y)
int *x, *y;
{
   int temp;
   temp = *x;
   *x = *y;
   *y = temp;
}
```

```
/***********************************************/
/* row_sorted - checks if sorted - returns BOOLEAN*/
/***********************************************/

BOOLEAN row_sorted()
{
   BOOLEAN sorted;
   int n;
   sorted = TRUE;
   n = 1;
   while ( (n<ROW_SIZE-1) && sorted )
   {
      if ( row[n+1] <= row[n] )
         sorted = FALSE;
      else
         n++;
   }
   return sorted;
}

/***********************************************/
/* initialise_row - puts values in row         */
/***********************************************/
void initialise_row()
{
   row[1] = 32;
   row[2] = 18;
   row[3] = 16;
   row[4] = 52;
   row[5] = 81;
}

/***********************************************/
/* print_instructions                          */
/***********************************************/
void print_instructions()
{
   printf("THE GAME OF REVERSE\n");
   printf("You can reverse a set of numbers,");
   printf(" starting from the left.\n");
   printf("The commands are:\n");
   printf("q - quit  i - instructions  r - reverse.\n");
   printf(" (after r you will be prompted for a number");
   printf("in the range 1 to %d)\n", ROW_SIZE -1 );
}
```

```
/***********************************************/
/* quit ends with number of attempts           */
/***********************************************/

void quit()
{
   printf("End of game - with %d goes\n", attempt_count);
}
/***********************************************/
/***********************************************/
```

Problems

1. get_valid_command() is a cut-down version of the full one (a stub). Modify it so that commands are rejected until a correct one appears.

2. The function rand() has no arguments and returns a random integer in the range 0 to MAX_INT (which depends on your particular compiler). Use this function to set initial values in the row array, but reject sequences already sorted, or which contain duplicates.

APPENDIX 1
VARIABLES IN RAM

A variable can be thought of as an electronic 'box', which holds a particular value. Each box has an address in RAM, but we refer to the variable by a name – e.g. x rather than 9000. The actual address of a variable is not important, and is decided by the C system software. In the following diagram, variables are shown arbitrarily at 9000 onwards. To access one of these variables takes around a microsecond.

Here are some C variable declarations, followed by assignment statements to give them a value:

```
/*  variables in ram  */
#include <stdio.h>
main()
{
    float x;
    int c,m,n,p;
    int a[4];
    int b[5];
    char d;
    static char animal[4]="cat"; /*declare AND initialise*/

/* now some assignments */
    x=3.6;
    c=-12345;
    p=100;
    a[2]=-84;
    n=100;
    d = '+';

/*   etc     */
```

Here is the RAM representation:

Address	Contents	name	
9000	3.59999	x	
9001	-12345	c	
etc	100	n	
		m	
	100	p	
		a[0]	
		a[1]	
	-84	a[2]	
		a[3]	
9009		b[0]	
		b[1]	
		b[2]	
		b[3]	
		b[4]	
	43	d	43 is ASCII code for '+'
9015	99	animal[0]	99 is ASCII code for 'c'
	97	animal[1]	
	116	animal[2]	
	0	animal[3]	the end-of-string marker

Note the following:

- If a variable has not yet been given a value, don't assume it is zero. It is likely to be a totally random unpredictable value.

- Float values are not guaranteed to be represented exactly. There will often be a slight inaccuracy – this is not a fault in the language, but arises because of the finite size of each box. Some float values need an infinite number of digits to represent them. (e.g. pi, or the answer to 2 divided by 3)

- Static arrays can be given a value when we declare them. If we didn't use static, we would have to use 4 assignment statements to accomplish the above.

- The size of each box depends on your computer – typical sizes are: 16 or 32 bits for ints, allowing approximately ± 32,000 and 2000,000,000 respectively.

- Total RAM size is usually given in 'megabytes'. A byte is usually an 8-bit region, and an integer needs at least two bytes. Typical RAM size is ½ to 5 megabytes.

- For convenience, the diagram shows all 'boxes' as being the same size. In reality, the space allocated to different types of variable will vary.

APPENDIX 2
LIBRARIES

Most C systems come with these libraries:

math string ctype stdio

Specific compilers may also have libraries targeted towards a particular machine – e.g. graphics, multi-programming, etc.

Here is a selection of functions from the above libraries.

■ Math #include <math.h> is needed.

The following functions operate with double-length float arguments and results, but because of C's type conversion, float values are accomodated as well. The functions are shown by example, using:

```
float f,g,r;
```

```
r = acos(f);     -  arc cos of f  (radians)
r = asin(f);     -  arc sin of f  (radians)
r = atan(f);     -  arc tan of f  (radians)
r = cos(f);      -  cosine of f  (radians)
r = sin(f);      -  sine of f  (radians)
r = tan(f);      -  tangent of f  (radians)
r = exp(f);      -  e to power f
r = log(f);      -  natural log of f
r = log10(f);    -  log (base 10) of f
r = pow(f,g);    -  f to power g
r = fabs(f);     -  absolute value of f
```

■ String #include <string.h> is needed.

Those functions not requiring a detailed knowledge of pointers are described in chapter 13.

■ Ctype #include <ctype.h> is needed.

The following macros (used exactly like functions) return a true/false 1/0 value. The functions are shown by example, using:
int r;
char c;

r = isalpha(c) – true if a letter
r = isupper(c) – true if an upper case letter
r = islower(c) – true if a lower case letter
r = isdigit(c) – true if a digit
r = isspace(c) – true if white space

See also chapter 9.

■ Stdio #include <stdio.h> is needed.

details of scanf() and printf() can be found in chapter 5, and file I/O is briefly described in chapter 15.

APPENDIX 3
RESERVED WORDS

In ANSI C, the following words are reserved ('booked–up') in the sense that you can't use them for variable or function names.

auto	break	case	char
const	continue	default	do
double	else	enum	extern
float	for	goto	if
int	long	register	return
short	signed	sizeof	static
unsigned	void	volatile	while

REFERENCES

Here are some selected additional texts:

Kernighan & Ritchie. The C Programming Language. Prentice – Hall.

Regarded as the 'bible', but not ideal for novices. The second edition uses ANSI C.

Kelly & Pohl. C by Dissection. Benjamin/Cummings

Farmer. The Intensive C Course. Chartwell – Bratt

A useful reference guide to ANSI C

Johnsonbaugh & Kalin. Applications Programming in C. Macmillan.

Big, but lots of examples.

Barclay. C Problem Solving and Programming. Prentice – Hall.

Good treatment of ANSI C to an advanced level.

INDEX

D

E

F

G

H

I

L

M

N

Learn C by video

with "C: The Effective Solution" from Chartwell-Bratt

This *excellent* video course assumes a basic knowledge of programming, and shows you how to write good programs, exploiting the capabilities of the latest language standard. It is illustrated with many practical examples. Based on courses given at Birkbeck College, University of London, the videos are professionally produced and presented in ten modules for flexibility of use.

In Industry

Many companies currently send staff out on expensive training courses. The disadvantages of these are that staff may remember only a fraction of the knowledge, may leave the company taking the training investment with them, and their productivity is lost during the course duration. This intensive video course is a once-only investment in the quality of knowledge and expertise in your company which, for a fraction of the cost of external courses, will provide a permanent and flexible training resource.

The course is supported by a very practically-orientated workbook and the successful textbook *The Intensive C Course* by Mick Farmer. A starter pack of 10 copies of each is included with every set of videos.

Course outline:

Unit 1: Setting Sail
- 1.1 Getting started
- 1.2 The language
- 1.3 The environment

Unit 2: Expressions and Statements
- 2.1 Operators
- 2.2 Conversions
- 2.3 Statements

Unit 3: Control Structures
- 3.1 Selection
- 3.2 Iteration
- 3.3 Jumping

Unit 4: Declarations
- 4.1 Types
- 4.2 Storage classes
- 4.3 Type definitions

Unit 5: Functions and Programs
- 5.1 Function
- 5.2 Programs

Unit 6: Arrays and Pointers
- 6.1 Arrays
- 6.2 Pointers
- 6.3 Memory management

Unit 7: Structures and Unions
- 7.1 Structures
- 7.2 Unions
- 7.3 Bit-fields

Unit 8: The Preprocessor
- 8.1 File Inclusion
- 8.2 Macro replacement
- 8.3 Conditional inclusion

Unit 9: Library
- 9.1 Headers
- 9.2 Content
- 9.3 Input/Output

Unit 10: Staying Afloat
- 10.1 Debugging
- 10.2 Portability

£850 + vat per set (10 thirty-minute Videos, 10 workbooks and 10 textbooks) - less 10% academic discount (A Preview VHS video available at £20 + vat, which may be deducted from the purchase price of the set)